Managing Unmanageable Students

To my husband, E. Raymond Adkins
To my children, Emily McEwan-Fujita and Patrick McEwan

EMA

To my husband, Stephen Kern
To my children, Justin and Simone

MD

Managing Unmanageable Students

Practical
Solutions
for
Administrators

Elaine K. McEwan
Mary Damer

CORWIN PRESS, INC.
A Sage Publications Company
Thousand Oaks, California

For information:

Corwin Press, Inc.
A Sage Publications Company
2455 Teller Road
Thousand Oaks, California 91320
E-mail: order@corwinpress.com

Sage Publications Ltd.
6 Bonhill Street
London EC2A 4PU
United Kingdom

Sage Publications India Pvt. Ltd.
M-32 Market
Greater Kailash I
New Delhi 110 048 India

Printed in the United States of America

Library of Congress Cataloging-in-Publication Data

McEwan, Elaine K., 1941—
    Managing unmanageable students: Practical solutions for administrators / by Elaine McEwan and Mary Damer.
        p. cm.
Includes bibliographical references.
ISBN 0-8039-6786-1 (cloth: alk. paper)
ISBN 0-8039-6787-X (pbk.: alk. paper)
 1. Problem children—Education—United States. 2. Behavior modification—United States. 3. Teacher-student relationships—United States. 4. Educational change—United States. I. Damer, Mary. II. Title.
    LC4801.5 .M39 2000
    371.5'8—dc21

                                                    99-050495

This book is printed on acid-free paper.

00 01 02 03 04 05 06   10 9 8 7 6 5 4 3 2

Production Editors: S. Marlene Head & Denise Santoyo
Editorial Assistant: Kristen L. Gibson
Typesetter: Rebecca Evans
Cover Designer: Tracy E. Miller

Contents

CHAPTER TWO

What You Need to Know

CHAPTER THREE

What You Need to Do

CHAPTER FOUR

Rewards and How to Use Them Effectively 77

CHAPTER FIVE

Punishment: What It Is and How to Make It Work for You 100

CHAPTER SIX

Effective Teachers Equal Effective Students: Critical Teaching Behaviors 115

List of Forms and Exhibits

Preface

As you lean back in your chair for a brief respite during another hectic day as a school principal, there is always one certainty. Before long your secretary will buzz to announce that Jason is here to see you. You won't need to ask, "Jason who?" You know him only too well. Jason tops your list of "10 Most Unmanageable Students." Oh, he is charming enough one-on-one, but he is routinely kicked out of class. You are not quite sure what happens behind the closed doors of his classroom. Jason and his teacher have very different perceptions about what goes on. When asked why he has been sent to your office, Jason will shrug his shoulders and give you a blank look. "Dunno," he'll say inscrutably. "She sent me." Of course you know who "she" is. Jason's teacher has documented a veritable dossier of his sins and would like to have him placed anywhere but in her classroom; reform school was her last suggestion. He does not seem like a bad kid, but he definitely falls into the unmanageable category. And, he is taking over your life.

Whether you are an elementary, middle, or high school principal, you have a variety of students like Jason in your school. They take your time and undermine your effectiveness as an instructional leader. Unfortunately, you are all alone at the top. There is nowhere to turn for help. Your staff expects you to leap tall buildings in a single bound, supply all of their curricular and instructional needs, and make sure that every student in your school is a model of self-discipline and decorum. Your hat rack is already filled with the multiple chapeaus you are wearing, but you will need to find room for one more after reading *Managing Unmanageable Students: Practical Solutions for Administrators*—the "behavior management consultant" hat.

We have written *Managing Unmanageable Students* to give you positive and productive ways to deal with students like Jason. The chapters ahead will provide the following:

1. Give you the tools you need to serve as a behavior management consultant to your staff.

2. Help you understand the relationship between effective instruction and student behavior.

3. Assist you in observing and counseling teachers in how to avoid no-win encounters with students.

4. Provide the forms you need for observing student behavior, completing a Functional Behavioral Assessment, and structuring workable interventions.

5. Unleash the power of school teams in managing unmanageable students.

6. Increase your effectiveness as an instructional leader.

We believe that all students can be successful in school if they experience effective instruction combined with appropriate structure and expectations.

Overview of the Contents

Chapter 1 introduces you to the three key players in the unmanageable student drama: the principal, the teacher, and the student. Each one of these players brings a set of behaviors to the "stage" that will impact the overall success of your efforts to manage unmanageable students. Consider first the 10 common mistakes that principals often make in dealing with unmanageable students. Before you even begin to think about the behavior of your students and teachers, examine whether your own behavior might be an unwitting contributor to the discipline and morale problems in your school. You will also meet 10 teacher types whose behaviors can contribute to escalating student discipline problems. Finally, you will be introduced to the 10 most common student behavior problems and discover how to deal with them using a proven problem-solving process.

Chapter 2 details the first four steps of the problem-solving model. Following our format will help your team easily develop a Functional Behavioral Assessment as mandated by the latest IDEA (Individuals With Disabilities Education Act). Chapter 3 sets forth the remaining six steps of the model. You will be introduced to research-based methods for modifying the student's classroom environment as well as his or her instruction and curriculum.

Chapters 4 and 5 contain essential information for developing successful behavioral intervention plans. They discuss the controversy surrounding behavior management, detail the specific advantages and pitfalls of rewards and punishments, and offer practical examples that your team can adapt.

Chapter 6 examines the critical teaching behaviors that impact student behavior and shows how "notching-up" the teaching performance of your staff will have a positive impact on unmanageable students.

Chapter 7 considers the importance of learning and shares some "magic" that can help your students improve not only their behavior but also their academic achievement.

Finally, Chapter 8 will give you 50 things you can do tomorrow. One or more of these ideas, when implemented by you and your staff members, will result in immediate benefits to your students and teachers.

We hope that after reading *Managing Unmanageable Students* you will feel empowered and energized. Our personal experiences have shown us and the available research demonstrates that student achievement is higher in schools where principals are perceived as strong instructional leaders. In environments where teachers are trained and supported, they will transmit their confidence and sense of efficacy to students. When students are respected and well taught, they will be more motivated to learn and interact with adults positively. General Norman Schwartzkopf said, "No organization is ever going to get better unless the leadership is willing to say that things need to be changed." You are the person to help unmanageable students be more positive and productive in school.

Acknowledgments

The authors would like to acknowledge the following reviewers:

Jodie Kratz, Learning Support Teacher
Swatara Junior High
Central Dauphin School District
Harrisburg, PA

Kady Rowe Garcia, Supervisor of Special Education
Missouri Dept. of Elementary and Secondary Education
Jefferson City, MO

Harriet Gould, Principal
Raymond Central Elementary
Valparaiso, NE

Bill Grobe, Junior Division Teacher
Mother Teresa Catholic School
Waterloo Catholic District School Board
Cambridge, Ontario

Jane Rice, Supervisor for Special Education
Spotsylvania County Schools
Spotsylvania, VA

Jon Rosell, Executive Vice President
Heartspring
Wichita, KS

Krystal D. Spurlock, Mentor Teacher
Clinton-Massie High School
Clarksville, OH

About the Authors

Elaine K. McEwan is a partner in the McEwan-Adkins Group, an educational consulting firm. She received her B.A. from Wheaton College, her M.A. in library science and her Ed.D. in educational administration from Northern Illinois University. She has been a teacher, librarian, elementary school principal, and assistant superintendent for instruction. McEwan is the author of more than two dozen books for parents, children, and educators, including *Attention Deficit Disorder* (1995); *Nobody Likes Me: Helping Your Child Make Friends* (1996); *When Kids Say No to School: Helping Students at Risk of Failure, Refusal, or Dropping Out* (1998); *Seven Steps to Effective Instructional Leadership* (1998); *The Principal's Guide to Attention Deficit Hyperactivity Disorder* (1998); *How to Deal With Parents Who Are Angry, Troubled, Afraid, or Just Plain Crazy* (1998); and *The Principal's Guide to Raising Reading Achievement* (1998).

Mary Damer has worked for the past 20 years as a behavior consultant in school districts throughout Illinois, collaborating with educators to develop individualized behavior management and to present workshops on behavior management issues. She has extensive experience in developing teacher training programs and currently is an instructor at Northern Illinois University, supervising student teachers in the special education program. She has been a teacher, the principal of a special education school, and a university administrator. She received her B.S. from Arizona State University and her M.Ed. from the University of Illinois at Chicago.

CHAPTER ONE

Managing Unmanageable Students

Who Needs to Change?

Three individuals have parts in our drama involving the unmanageable student: the principal, the teacher, and the student. Although the settings and supporting cast change frequently in the ongoing vignettes that compose this masterpiece of suspense and action, one individual always plays a central role: the school principal.

In a typical week you act as a facilitator, disciplinarian, or even just a frustrated bystander. You are caught up in this drama more frequently than you should be, your time consumed by what seem to be petty arguments, vague complaints, and power struggles between teachers and students. You may also play an unintended part, that of contributor to the "problem."

An often heard maxim in behavioral psychology goes like this: "If you want to change someone's behavior, then first change your own." As building principals, we (Elaine and Mary) did our share of changing our personal behavior to impact that of our faculty and students. We have also used the powerful tool of personal change to motivate our children and spouses to change their ways. As with all meaningful learning, changing our own well-entrenched behavior patterns was at times difficult and even painful.

Perhaps the thought of changing your leadership style or behavior to better manage the behavior of unmanageable children has not occurred to you. Maybe you are even surprised that we would dare to suggest something so bold. After all, you are mumbling to yourself, "I bought this book to get ideas, not get blamed." Be assured, you will be introduced to the ideas you are seeking in just a moment. But, if you are interested in working behavioral miracles in unmanageable children and you expect teachers to also change their behavior, figure out right from the start if you need to change your personal ways of doing business as well. Your staff, students, and parent community probably won't be standing in line to tell you the truth about yourself. Instead, they will be inexplicably resistant to change unless they sense that you are willing to turn over a new leaf too.

Are You a Part of the Problem or a Part of the Solution?

Here are some dreadful mistakes that building principals unknowingly make. These attitudes and behaviors contribute to the epidemic of unmanageable students we are seeing in today's schools.

The Administrivia Administrator

This principal spends most of his time dealing with paperwork and approaches disruptive students as items on a "to-do" list: "move 'em in, move 'em out." Unmanageable students receive a canned lecture they have heard on multiple occasions before they are summarily sent back to their classrooms. When teachers ask students what happened in the principal's office, they usually reply, "Nuthin'." And they have got it just about right.

It Is Not in My Job Description

This principal never attends team meetings in which student behavior is discussed. If a behavior management consultant is hired to assist in solving behavioral problems, this principal is never available to offer back up, suggestions, follow-through, or support. After all, managing unmanageable students is someone else's responsibility.

Marine Drill Instructor

This principal is punitive and closed-minded. There is only one way to handle an unmanageable student: back the teacher and bluster. The student's viewpoint is never considered. This principal nostalgically wishes for a return to the days when corporal punishment was permitted. "That old paddle would resolve these bothersome discipline problems."

Psychotherapist

This principal is sympathetic, empathetic, and "touchy-feely" to a fault. An unmanageable student will always be accorded the benefit of the doubt, will never be held accountable for his or her actions, and will be sent back to class with a hug or a pat on the back. Unmanageable students sometimes act out in class in anticipation of increased positive attention from this principal.

"We Want Our Students to Be Intrinsically Motivated"

This principal offers no positive feedback to either teachers or students for improved classroom behavior. She believes firmly that students should be intrinsically motivated and refuses to become involved in behavior management programs that include rewards. This principal believes that praising teachers or students will lead to a decrease in performance standards and never commends anyone for a job well done.

The Invisible Presence

In contrast to the strong instructional leader whose visible presence provides support and encouragement for teachers and students, this principal is rarely seen in classrooms, on the playground, or at after-school activities. The door to this principal's office is usually shut, guarded by a watchful secretary who invariably says that he or she is busy.

The Latest Innovation Is the Miracle Solution

This principal swings with the educational pendulum. The latest instructional trends are sure to be recommended as the solution to behavior problems in this principal's school. Staff members who approach this principal about an unmanageable student's behavior are likely to receive an oration related to the "fad-of-the-month." "Teach to this student's multiple intelligences," or "Use more cooperative groups" are possible responses.

It Is All Your Fault

This principal blames parents for all of the problems that students have. A divorce, the mother's anger, and/or the long hours that parents work are insurmountable problems for the student that the school cannot possibly resolve. This attitude absolves everyone, including the principal, of any responsibility.

Hear No Evil, See No Evil

This principal either does not recognize behavioral problems or is power-less to do anything about the poor instruction or lax classroom manage-ment that create low morale and disastrous student achievement.

Get This Child Out of My Building

This principal's approach screams, "Get this child out of my hair and send him or her somewhere else." If the child is in a regular classroom, this principal thinks that removing the child to the special education class-room will resolve the problem.

To this principal, a behavior problem is synonymous with a behavior disorder. If the child poses a problem in the special education classroom, then the solution is to send the child to an alternative school building. If this principal calls in a behavior consultant, he expects the behavior con-sultant to facilitate the student's move out of the school. The only accept-able solution is one that gets rid of the student.

If you recognize yourself in one or more of these descriptions, reflect on how you might change, although changing your own behavior is only the first step toward managing unmanageable students. The second step requires taking a serious look at your teaching staff.

Troublesome Teachers Can Lead to Troublesome Students

If your school is located in the mythical Minnesota town of Lake Wobegon, popularized by humorist Garrison Keilor, you will seldom en-counter unmanageable teachers. In Lake Wobegon, every staff member views the world in an objective and organized fashion, managing their classrooms with energy and effectiveness. These paragons of pedagogical practice rarely send disruptive students to the principal's office, being far more likely to resolve discipline problems by themselves or prevent them in the first place with high expectations, structure, and superior teaching.

Most of us live in the real world, however, where we are always faced with a few teachers who make our lives challenging because of their atti-tudes and behaviors. See if any of these teachers are currently members of your staff. They can often be as unmanageable as their students are.

Burned-Out at 35

This teacher is thinking about everything except what is happening in the classroom. With two young children plus master's level courses three times a week, this teacher invariably volunteers to direct the holiday program. This teacher moves through her day in a daze of fatigue and disorientation. You have recently discovered that she has not returned homework assignments for weeks.

My Classroom Is Not a Fishbowl

This teacher is uncomfortable whenever another adult enters his classroom. Parent volunteers are tolerated rather than encouraged. The mantle of disapproving silence is so intense when you drop in for visits that you find yourself avoiding this classroom. This teacher would have to be on the verge of a nervous collapse before ever asking for assistance from anyone.

If Only

This teacher scapegoats one student each year—sometimes a taller, brighter, or more outspoken one, but frequently a boy or a minority student. If only this student were not difficult . . . the class would be further in the curriculum, other students would be more on task, or the lesson plans would be more organized. This teacher holds forth regularly on the character flaws of the targeted student, one in a succession of problematic students she always seems to have. No matter how carefully you design the class lists, a culprit will emerge by mid-September. The pattern is always the same. Is the student really disruptive, or does the teacher trigger the behavior?

First to Any Fad

You are reminded of a chameleon when you observe how this teacher revamps the entire classroom after attending the latest inservice or graduate class. Last year, this teacher attempted to stimulate both sides of the students' brains by transforming the classroom into a rain forest complete with sound effects and hanging vines. This year, he is scheduling every subject at a different time each day in order to teach to the students' varying biological clocks. The only constant with "First to Any Fad" is innovation, and although you respect creativity, you find many of the new ideas counterproductive.

Put on a Show

This teacher only carries out your suggestions when you are observing in the classroom. You have tried on three different occasions to see the disruptive student in action, but you have only observed angelic behavior. You suspect that the student she has referred would always be on-task if the teacher consistently taught this well, but you also know that you are seeing a once-in-a-lifetime Academy Award-winning performance. This teacher is so adept at putting on the costume for theatricals that when you slip into the classroom unannounced, the activity suddenly changes as even the students look astonished. Sometimes you can outwait this teacher if you sit in the classroom long enough. When lesson plans have not been developed and the teacher is not accustomed to positively acknowledging students, it is hard to keep the show going for more than an hour and a half. You grow weary just thinking of what you will have to do to unmask the charade.

What Month Is It?

The hurricane decor of this classroom provides a clue to this teacher's disorganization. The gradebook disappeared last week and math is only taught sporadically. This agreeable, well-meaning individual always intends to "do it," but never quite manages to follow through.

The Control Freak

This teacher is a power struggle waiting to happen. Unmanageable students and control-freak teachers mix like oil and water. They bring out the worst in each other and it is always a lose-lose scenario. This teacher must win every battle, be right every time, and always bring students to their knees in abject surrender. This teacher will go to any lengths to substantiate the righteousness of his position and interprets any use of modifications or accommodations as giving in.

It Is Not My Problem

This teacher wants the problem to disappear as quickly as possible. She is rooted in teaching the "Father Knows Best" classroom of the 50s and expects that students' behavior will conform. Resolving the problem caused by an unmanageable student means only one thing for this teacher—send the child to special education and let them "fix it." Resistant to analyzing personal teaching behavior or making adaptations, this teacher is fixated on eliminating the child from the classroom. The only discussion this teacher wants to hear is one to determine where the student should go next.

It Is Not in My Job Description (in the Contract)

This teacher has every school board policy, the teacher handbook, and the negotiated contract memorized. Don't ask him to do anything that might require extra work, a special meeting, or creativity. This teacher will have you sitting in a grievance hearing faster than you can swivel your chair.

I Am Really Not Sure What the Problem Is

This teacher views the world as an ever-changing collage and misses the patterns. When you ask this teacher what the unmanageable student has done to cause the disruption, she will talk about the student's family troubles, an incident that happened in the classroom last week, and/or what last year's teacher said in the teacher's lounge about the student. This teacher is unable to see the forest for the trees, and, because he or she has not clearly identified the disruptive behaviors, cannot begin to formulate ideas about what triggers them.

The Top 10 Behavior Problems of Today's Students

Perhaps your discipline log is filled with hundreds of seemingly unique behavior problems, each one perpetrated by a student slightly more creative than the last. Our 10 problems may strike you as rather dull and pedestrian, hardly worthy of top billing in comparison to your students' exploits of derring-do. But, strip away the colorful details and you will find that your incidents are merely variations. You might also question the need for stating the seemingly obvious positive counterpart to each negative behavior that we have included in our descriptions. However, we have found in our consultations with principals and teachers that the inability to define a student's behavior and its positive counterpart in precise behavioral terms is the major stumbling block to developing a cogent behavior plan.

Dishonesty is omitted from the list because its associated behaviors do not meet the primary prerequisite for modification by a typical behavior management plan: they are not readily observable. Lying, cheating, and stealing are serious problems and cannot be ignored. If you encounter students with continuing patterns of dishonesty, the assistance of a therapist or counselor is essential. The first step is determining the cause of the dishonesty; the second step is helping the student to accept responsibility and make restitution (McEwan, 1996). This is a long-term and complex process that is not amenable to behavioral interventions of the type we are describing.

In contrast, our top 10 behavior problems are all responsive to elimination using a well-conceived behavior intervention. The top 10 problems can, in fact, be almost totally eliminated from your school campus if you and your teachers are willing to do what it takes. Educators as a group are quick to establish zero-tolerance policies for guns, drugs, and gang activities, actions that garner favorable press and paint us as "no-nonsense" disciplinarians, but, if you do not take the same tough stance against physical aggression, harassment, threatening language, and abusive treatment of peers and teachers, you are sending the wrong message to students and teachers. Tackling the "small stuff" while it is still manageable will foster a school environment in which the catastrophic problems are far less likely to occur.

Leaving School Grounds

Leaving the school grounds (e.g., classroom, playground area, or school building) is a dangerous behavior that puts school staff in legal jeopardy and poses a danger to the student. Students who engage in this behavior need to learn to stay in the required area.

Physical Aggression Toward Others
With Hands, Feet, and/or Objects

This category includes hitting, pushing, tripping, biting, choking an individual, or jabbing an individual with an object (e.g., ruler, stick, or weapon). Also included are behaviors such as throwing ice or rocks at someone or destroying their possessions. Students who engage in these behaviors need to learn to respect others and keep their hands, feet, and objects to themselves.

Disturbing Others With Hands,
Feet, and/or Objects

This behavior is similar to the physical aggression behaviors, but the student's intention does not appear to be malicious. This disruptive behavior is more likely to be displayed by a student who is hyperactive or who lacks the necessary social skills to respect the space of others. Included in this are touching other students' possessions, taking others' materials, or inappropriately touching other students or their desks. Students who engage in these behaviors also need to learn to respect other people, and keep hands, feet, and objects to themselves.

Use of Disrespectful and/or Threatening Language

This category includes swearing, threats, name calling, demeaning comments, verbal insults, or obvious rude comments not appropriate in the classroom setting. These comments may be directed to staff or to other students. Students who engage in this behavior need to learn appropriate negotiation strategies and respectful talking with classmates, the teachers, and/or other staff members.

Inappropriate Use of School Materials

This set of behaviors includes crumpling work papers that the teacher has handed out, breaking pencils, throwing objects, kicking furniture, using materials taken without permission from the teacher's desk, writing on the walls, or putting objects into toilets. Students who engage in these behaviors need to learn to take care of school materials.

Talking Out in Class

This behavior includes speaking out without permission during a time when the teacher's rules clearly specify that students must receive permission to talk. Also included is interrupting the teacher or another student who has been recognized to talk during a lesson. Students who engage in these behaviors need to learn to wait for conversation turns.

Out-of-Seat Behavior

This category includes leaving one's seat without the teacher's permission if that is one of the classroom rules. If students were allowed to rise from their desks and stretch or get materials independently, out-of-seat behavior would occur when the student wandered outside of an arm's touch of the desk to engage in nonpurposeful activity. Students who engage in this behavior need to learn to stay in the desk area unless work requires movement.

Noncompliance With Teacher's Requests and Directions

This set of behaviors refers to any type of observable refusal to follow the teacher's instructions or directions. This behavior includes putting one's head on the desk in response to the teacher's request to work, verbally refusing to follow the teacher's instructions, or physically refusing to follow the teacher's directions to move. Students who engage in this behavior need to learn to follow the teacher's directions.

Inability to Work Independently Without Adult Intervention

This behavior occurs when a student does not work on individual assignments or read specified materials when the teacher or another adult is not giving direct one-to-one attention. This behavior includes staring into space, doing a different activity than the specified one, and unpurposeful manipulation of materials at desk. Students who engage in this behavior need to learn to work independently on a learning task.

Nondisruptive Disorganized Behaviors

This set of behaviors includes noncompletion of homework, slow rate of work completion, inability to find required materials in desk, excessive dawdling during transition periods, and failure to follow more complicated instructions. Students who engage in this behavior need to learn organizational and school survival skills.

We hope that you are beginning to appreciate that managing unmanageable students is a serious learning task for everyone: principal, teacher, and especially the student. No one will emerge unchanged from the problem-solving process we suggest.

A Problem-Solving Process That Works

Following is a brief overview of the 10-step problem-solving process that we have developed and used during our careers. Chapters 2 and 3 will discuss each step in more detail and offer specific examples and strategies.

Step 1: What Is the Critical Problem?

Before you can help your staff to resolve a student's chronic discipline problem, analyze exactly what is happening and why. Is the student's unmanageable behavior a "high priority" behavior requiring crisis intervention? What solutions has the teacher already implemented to resolve the discipline problem, and why haven't they worked? What are the possible triggers to the unmanageable behavior? Is the student in question truly unmanageable?

Sometimes when a teacher has a discipline problem involving the whole class, he or she will unknowingly blame the disruption on the tallest student, the wiggliest student, or a minority student. Your analysis will ensure that a seemingly unmanageable student is not made a scapegoat because of an ineffective teacher's overall lack of classroom management skills.

Step 2: Where, When, and How Often Is the Behavior Occurring?

Once you have defined the specific behavior problem to be addressed, work with your staff to gather information about its occurrence. Eventually, you will expect your staff members to collect their own preliminary data and bring it to the initial discussion. In the beginning, however, they will need encouragement and training to help them collect useful information. Educators, especially teachers, are often resistant to collecting data methodically; they often place more confidence in their "feelings" about what is happening. However, a discussion between a principal and teacher will always be more productive if the teacher can provide information such as the following:

> Roald is giving me problems during math class. He gets out of his seat and walks over to other students and interferes with their work. He also makes faces or tries to talk about TV shows he has watched. Yesterday, I counted six disruptions during class. I've tried reminding him of the rules, sternly talking to him, and taking away five minutes of his recess time.

When the teacher can provide factual data about the precise behaviors that are occurring, how often they are occurring, and what interventions he or she has already tried, the principal and school team will have the necessary information to start planning an intervention. Postponing any discussion until the teacher supplies the data to support his or her concerns is a good way to ensure that teachers always come prepared.

Remind yourself and the teachers who want to skip this step of its importance in the problem-solving process. For example, a training manual explaining the TQM (Total Quality Management) problem-solving philosophy reminds us that "views not backed by data are more likely to include personal opinions, exaggeration and mistaken impressions" (Walton, 1986, p. 96). Introduce your staff to the practical, easy data collection tools we recommend in Chapter 2. Resolving a behavior problem can only be done properly when everyone has objective information.

Step 3: What Do the Parents and the Student Think?

Aim for a collaborative relationship with the parents of a difficult student from the very beginning. Gaining parental input and support will save you time as well as the possible associated costs of litigation. The parents of an unmanageable child have often had a history of negative communication with school staff. At some point in the child's school career, a teacher may have documented every behavioral infraction of which their child was guilty. Or, the parents may have been frequently called at work and directed to "do something" about their child's behavior. The parents of a typical unmanageable child may never have been the recipients of a single complimentary or supportive statement about their child. Their stomachs knot when a call comes from school personnel because it invariably portends bad news. Parents of unmanageable students then begin to avoid the school, often canceling scheduled meetings because of sudden "emergencies." The school is perceived as an adversary, an institution "out to get" them and their child.

Whenever a child moves into your district, you inherit his or her entire school history. For example, if the previous district worked in close partnership with the parents, you will reap the benefits. If a prior administrator or teacher callously blamed the child's school problems on the parents, you will be guilty by association. As soon as you recognize a potential problem with an unmanageable student, begin to cultivate a positive relationship with the parents. Most parents will appreciate the extra time you spend in developing a motivational plan or making curricular and instructional changes to help their child be more successful in school. We often receive appreciative notes from parents who were initially hostile toward the school staff, but came to recognize and affirm our efforts to treat them with respect. By involving the parents and child in the problem-solving process, you will increase the quality of the intervention plan you design as well as its potential for success. Take care, however, to avoid personally intrusive questions or confrontational attitudes. You will need these parents on your side!

Step 4: What Patterns Emerge From Examining the Data?

Collate the information collected from everyone's observations. Then, look for patterns that might explain what is triggering the behaviors. Does the student become disruptive only after the teacher assigns independent work? Is the student most problematic during less-supervised times such as recess, lunch, and hall passing periods? Do the other students in the class laugh every time the student calls out profanities? Do you find that even as an observer, the teacher's lack of structure makes you uneasy or nervous? Does the student become most disruptive when sitting on the rug, elbow to elbow with the other classmates? Does the teacher ignore the student's misbehavior until it becomes explosive? Finding obvious patterns to a student's misbehavior will help you "connect the dots," hence creating a complete picture of what is happening.

Step 5: Figure Out What Needs to Change: Environmental, Instructional, and Curricular Adaptations

Research supports the underlying thesis of our problem-solving process; the heart of successful behavior management is good instruction. Effective teaching becomes an even more essential variable for managing student behavior when one or more of the following conditions is present: (a) a student has a particularly chaotic home environment, (b) a student's learning problems are extensive and complex, or (c) a student's behavior is especially impulsive.

If Carla, the fourth grader who was constantly in your office last year, poses no problem in fifth grade, chances are that her teacher this year is more skillful. If you observe Carla, you are likely to see her current teacher employing teaching methods that reflect the most valid research practices. Whenever you have a teacher on your staff who is complaining that a student who posed no problems last year is now a noncompliant rule-breaker, take a close look at that teacher's instructional methods. You may find important clues to the student's sudden misbehavior in the quality of the teacher's instruction.

Instructional practices derived from specific curriculum designs can also directly affect student behavior. Many of the constructivist curricular innovations of the past 10 years that were created to develop hands-on, cooperative learning, and student-centered environments often produced unintended results for children who are distractible, impulsive, or less motivated toward school.

Consider the following observation notes based on a classroom observation of two sixth graders in a math class.

The students are seated five to a table. They are manipulating small blocks into patterns in order to invent a method of multiplying fractions. Only two students in the class appear to have understood the concept. Other students seem confused and frustrated. The teacher is unable to assist the students who are having difficulty and still monitor the other students. The instant she pauses to provide assistance to one table of students, a craps game begins on the other side of the room with several students exchanging pennies for the blocks they are now flicking across a finish line. One of the two referred students is walking around the classroom, seemingly to avoid the assigned task; the other unmanageable student has lined up his blocks like a train.

The frustration and lack of structure engendered by this activity have created multiple, predictable triggers to unmanageable behavior. No behavior intervention plan will succeed in a classroom where the assigned task is as frustrating as this one is, and the activities are as unstructured as these activities are.

Step 6: Make a Hypothesis About the Function/Purpose of the Behavior

A careful examination of the patterns you have identified, the classroom environment, and instruction will help you develop a hypothesis about the function(s) or purpose(s) of the student's misbehavior. Two students may use the same disruptive behavior for completely different reasons. Crystal may be hitting other students in the classroom as revenge because she is bullied on the playground. The function of her aggression appears to be revenge-seeking. Frank may also be hitting other students in the classroom, but he appears to enjoy the teacher's negative attention along with the consequence of being sent out of the classroom during oral reading. His aggressive behavior looks as if it might be a result of his attention-seeking combined with a lack of skills in reading grade-level text.

The behavior intervention that your team develops will be more effective if you take into account your hypothesis about what function(s) the student's behavior is serving. Although the actual behavior of Crystal and Frank looks identical, the purpose of their behavior differs significantly. Any behavior intervention you develop will need to reflect those differences.

By the time you are finished with Steps 1 through 6, you have completed a Functional Behavioral Assessment, thereby increasing the probability of successfully resolving a student's disruptive behavior and minimizing guesswork. This factual information that your staff has gathered regarding when and where the disruptive behavior is occurring, what function the behavior serves for the student, and what patterns are associated with the behavior will serve as the basis for your decisions in Steps 7 through 10.

Step 7: Develop a Plan

Now it's time to develop a plan of action. You will always ensure a higher rate of success in resolving a student's unmanageable behaviors if your plan includes several possible ideas for implementation. Researchers typically change only one variable at a time, such as trying a reinforcement program, but practitioners need results much faster. Attacking the problem from a number of perspectives while taking care not to overload the teacher will give you the best chance to eliminate the unmanageable behavior.

Put together a team of three or four staff members to sit down and plan the actual changes that might resolve the student's behavior problems. Set aside at least an hour to formulate your plan. The authors of *The Wisdom of Teams: Creating the High-Performance Organization* (Katzenbach & Smith, 1983) remind us that "Teams outperform individuals acting alone . . . especially when performance requires multiple skills, judgments, and experiences" (p. 9). Depending on the skills of the other team members, you might serve as either the team leader or in a more supportive role as the facilitator.

Step 8: Implement the Plan

Unless the student's unmanageable behaviors escalate immediately following the onset of implementation, allow 3 to 4 weeks to assess the effectiveness of proposed changes. During this time, your most important responsibility will be monitoring the plan. Are teachers carrying out the proposed changes consistently? Is one of the changes backfiring? Is the "criticism trap" you identified in the classroom gone for good? Many teachers will be heartened by the questions you ask and the monitoring you provide, viewing them ultimately as supportive. Other teachers will feel threatened. Use all of your communication skills to change that misinterpretation.

Step 9: Figure Out If the Plan Has Worked and Change It If Necessary

As part of the initial plan, your team will have determined how to regularly collect data to ensure a high level of accountability. Without data, mistakes in judgment regarding the effectiveness of the plan can occur. For example, if a student is making steady, but almost imperceptible progress, a team might erroneously conclude that the plan did not work. More infrequently, if a team is heavily invested in the progress of the student, the opposite conclusion could be reached. For example, everyone might conclude that the student is more compliant, when actually there has been no change. Only the presence of objective data will convincingly demonstrate the plan's effectiveness. Is the student more on-task at the end of the month? Have more homework papers been completed? Has the student been keeping hands and feet to self a greater majority of the time? When the team can answer these questions with supportive data, there will be no doubt about progress or a lack of it.

We always feel fortunate when a plan to resolve unmanageable behaviors accomplishes its goals the first time. More often than not, however, the team will need to fine-tune the plan. Perhaps after a week, John could care less about earning extra gym time for work completion. He obviously needs a different incentive. Or, the staff now realizes that John is totally frustrated with division problems because he is still not fluent with subtraction. Until a curricular change is made, John will not be able to finish his assignments.

Sometimes the team leader will discover that the plan was not practical because of the number of students in the teacher's classroom. Sometimes a team member has suggested that a teacher award a child a point every 10 minutes for keeping his arms and legs to himself, only to realize that in a large classroom, any time interval less than 20 minutes is unworkable. The follow-up team meeting allows for changes to the plan while keeping those adaptations that have worked.

When a team has fine-tuned the original plan several times and the student's behavior continues to escalate, the team must change its focus and explore other options.

Step 10: Decide What to Do Next

When we devise a plan to resolve a student's unmanageable behavior, we want to eliminate the unwanted behavior, but we also eventually want to wean the student from the special incentives or organizational charts that have supplied the needed motivation. We risk making the student dependent on earning points or on meeting with the teacher at his locker every day if we do not systematically plan how to fade out those strategies. The fading-out process can take an extended period for the student who has presented severe problems, but unless the student is slowly and gradually weaned from the successful interventions, he or she is not likely to maintain the improved behavior when the interventions are withdrawn. Team meetings to fine-tune the fading process will not require a great deal of time, but will ensure that the student can eventually manage his own behavior without the intense support of others.

This brief introduction to our 10-step problem-solving process is only the beginning. Chapter 2 provides specific instructions to help you collect the data you will need to develop a successful intervention plan (Steps 1 through 4), whereas Chapter 3 includes detailed information about developing and implementing the plan (Steps 5 through 10).

CHAPTER TWO

What You Need to Know

Dealing with unmanageable students can be the most frustrating and time-consuming aspect of your principalship, or it can be one of the most rewarding and satisfying experiences. The difference lies in your approach to handling the problems. Do you address them in a haphazard and disorganized fashion? Do you try to sweep them under the rug or perhaps attempt to handle them on your own? If so, then you are no doubt experiencing discouragement and failure. The most effective way to create success for your seemingly unmanageable students is to use the step-by-step, organized, and data-driven process we introduced in Chapter 1. Although our problem-solving model does not come with a money-back guarantee, it is backed by our years of experience as administrators (Mary and Elaine) and as a behavior management consultant (Mary). The Behavior Intervention Planning Form (Form 2.1) will help you maintain an adequate paper trail and includes all of the crucial steps in the problem-solving process. The form's sidebars highlight how effective behavior intervention planning begins with a Functional Behavioral Assessment (Numbers 1, 2, and 3), which lays the groundwork for developing the actual Behavior Intervention (Numbers 4 and 5).

At this point in your reading, you may be asking, why not move immediately to Number 4 on the Behavior Intervention Plan and eliminate the longer planning process? After all, time is of the essence when dealing with an unmanageable student and you need an action plan as quickly as possible.

Not only is the completion of a Functional Behavioral Assessment "best practice" when developing a behavior intervention, but as of July 1, 1998, your school district is mandated by the reauthorization of the Individuals With Disabilities Education Act (IDEA; 1997) to include one in the Individual Educational Plan (IEP) of any student requiring special education services whose behavior impedes their learning or the learning of others. The authors of "Functional Behavioral Assessment: The Link Between Problem Behavior and Effective Intervention in Schools" (Miller, Tansy, & Hughes, 1998) explain the new mandate.

		Date Completed
Functional Behavioral Assessment	Student: Teacher(s): Date: Person Completing Form:	

	1. Define problem: Principal meets with teacher(s)/other involved school staff.
	  A. Describe undesirable target behavior(s) to decrease and determine whether of high, medium, or low priority.
	  B. Describe desirable target behavior(s) to increase.
	  C. Describe classroom rules that teacher has established.
	  D. Describe interventions that the staff have already tried.
	  E. Describe times of day when the problem is occurring.
	  F. Interview student. (optional)
	  G. If student takes medication, distribute fact sheet about medicine and related side effects. (if applicable)	

	2. Observe problem: Teacher keeps record of occurrences of target disruptive behavior(s). Principal and other school staff observe student in situation where discipline problems most frequently occur.
	  A. Record how often the target disruptive behavior occurs, noting what happened before and after the behavior.
	  B. Record percentage of time student is on-task.
	  C. Record praise/critical comments ratio in classroom.
	  D. Complete Motivation Analysis Form (2.8) with parents.
	  E. Interface with medical professionals. (if applicable)
	  F. Complete Before-and-After Form(s) 2.9.	

	3. Analyze problem: Before the team meeting, each staff member should examine data and come prepared to suggest hypotheses about:
	  A. What curriculum demands and environmental factors could be triggering the target disruptive behavior(s)?
	  B. What teacher behavior could be triggering or maintaining the target disruptive behavior(s)?
	  C. What are the frequent patterns associated with the target disruptive behavior(s)?
	  D. Complete the Behavior Function Grid, Form 3.2.	

Behavior Intervention	4. Develop intervention plan: School team will meet to develop a behavior intervention plan and curricular/instructional adaptations based on their analysis.
	  A. Determine curricular and instructional adaptations.
	  B. Plan behavior intervention. (optional)
	  C. Establish team responsibilities.
	  D. Set timetable for revision.	

	5. Evaluate effectiveness of plan and determine follow-up activities.	

McEwan, E., & Damer, M. *Managing Unmanageable Students: Practical Solutions for Administrators.*
© 2000, Corwin Press, Inc.

FORM 2.1   Behavior Intervention Planning Form

[T]he local education agency is mandated to conduct an FBA (Functional Behavioral Assessment) and develop a BIP (Behavior Intervention Plan) when the behavior results in a suspension of more than ten days, as this is considered a violation of a student's right to a free and appropriate public education. This may include out-of-school suspensions in which the student is asked to stay at home during the school day, in-school suspensions in which the student is not allowed to attend his or her regular schedule of classes but still attends school, or a combination of in-school and out-of-school suspensions. This also includes interim placements for students found with weapons or drugs on a school campus and considerations of expulsion from a school district. The pivotal issue with regard to suspension is that the student has been or is being considered for removal from the current educational placement for more than ten days. It is clear that an FBA and a BIP is mandated at this point.

If you have followed our problem-solving process with the students who have unmanageable behaviors in your building, you will not be caught in an rapidly escalating pressure cooker crisis, having to pull support staff and teachers from their current duties in order to develop an emergency Functional Behavioral Assessment. Not only will you have reduced the number of crisis situations that take place in your school, but when they do occur, a completed Functional Behavioral Assessment will already be a part of the student's file or IEP.

Steps 1 through 4 of our problem-solving process deal with what you need to know to get the job done. By the time you have finished them, you will have worked your way through the first two categories on the Behavior Intervention Planning Form 2.1. Do not skip these important information-gathering steps.

The Problem-Solving Process: Steps 1 Through 4

Step 1: What Is the Critical Problem?

Define the Problem

Consider the usual course of events. Your first introduction to an unmanageable student is often his or her sudden appearance in the outer office. The body language says it all. This student has been "kicked out" of class. When asked why they sent a student to your office, many teachers will tell you that the student was disruptive, rude, or aggressive. These vague answers do not provide the details that are needed for resolution. Pinpoint exactly what behavior caused the student to be banned from the lunchroom for a week. Determine precisely what the student did that caused the bus driver to file three complaints last month. Ascertain specifically what the student did to be ejected from language arts class. Unless you know all of the details about a student's full range of problem behaviors, you cannot develop a plan to resolve them.

A well-organized teacher who is able to reflect on his or her teaching and the student's behavior as they interact can readily describe a student's undesirable behavior as requested in Number 1A of the Behavior Intervention Planning Form. But, if you are resolving a behavior problem with a vague and nonspecific teacher, the information-gathering process will be more time consuming.

Begin your conversation by asking probing questions, pausing when distracting factors (e.g., discussion of the student's home dynamics or clothes the student wore last week) interfere with the process. Reassure the teacher that although other factors exist, you must first identify exactly what this child is doing. Occasionally, a teacher is so focused on a global view of the unmanageable student that you will not be able to find out exactly what the student is doing unless you spend several periods of time observing the student personally. However, if your probing questions can bring the teacher to identify the specific problem behaviors, you will save valuable time. If necessary, show the list of top 10 student problems to the teacher and ask which problems the student exhibits.

Assess the Student's Medical History and Special Education Status

A first step toward defining the problem of any student must include assessing his or her medical history. If a student is taking medication at school, some communication with the physician has no doubt already taken place (Form 2.2, School Medication Authorization Form), but without the close follow-up of the school nurse, teachers may be unaware of this important information. One of the school nurse's responsibilities is the routine preparation of informational sheets for staff members describing any medications the student is taking (either at school or at home) along with a listing of any other health-related conditions (see Exhibit 2.1 for a sample Medication Fact Sheet). Teachers should be periodically asked to complete a Medication Follow-Up Report (Form 2.3), to determine if behavioral problems may be the results of medication side effects.

A perennial problem for school health officials is the reluctance or refusal of students to take their medication at school. A pattern of irregular medication dosages can result in disruptive behavior. Another responsibility of the school nurse is to make sure that students take their medications on time. The following strategies have been effective with many students:

- Assign a staff member (e.g., secretary, health aide) to remind the student to take medication.

(text continues on page 26)

Student's Name: _____ School: _____ Grade: _____

Address: _____

Birth Date: _____ Telephone Number: _____

I, _____ parent or guardian of_____ hereby authorize XYZ School District and its
employees and agents, on my behalf and stead, to administer to my child, (or to allow my child to self-
administer, while under the supervision of the employees and agents of the School District,) lawfully
prescribed medication in the manner described below. I further acknowledge and agree that, when the
lawfully prescribed medication is so administered, I waive any claims I have against the School District, its
employees and agents arising out of the administration of said medication. In addition, I agree to indemnify
and hold harmless the School District, its employees and agents, as a group or individually from and
against any and all claims, damages, causes of action or injuries, including reasonable attorney's fees and
costs expended in defense thereof, incurred or resulting from the administration of said medication.

_____

Parent or Guardian Signature   Date

To Be Completed by the Student's Physician:

Name of Medication: _____

Dosage:_____ Time: _____

Type of Disease or Illness: _____

Must this medication be administered during the school day in order to allow the child to attend school?

        Yes No

Are there any side effects to the medication? Yes No

If yes, please specify:

Can this child self-administer medication on field trip?   Yes No

_____

Doctor's Name (please print)   Doctor's Signature

_____

Address

_____

Telephone Number   Emergency Telephone Number

McEwan, E., & Damer, M. *Managing Unmanageable Students: Practical Solutions for Administrators.*
© 2000, Corwin Press, Inc.

Reprinted by permission of West Chicago Elementary District #33, West Chicago, Illinois. Readers may
reproduce this document for their professional use.

FORM 2.2 School Medication Authorization Form

Ritalin™

The most commonly used medication to treat ADHD is the psychostimulant Ritalin™ (methylphenidate hydrochloride). Note that the capitalized medication is a trademarked brand name, and the name following is the generic drug. Ritalin™ is most often prescribed for children 6 years of age and older.

Ritalin™ is not recommended if the following conditions exist: high generalized anxiety, motor tics or a family history of Tourette syndrome, thought disturbances, parents or adolescent siblings who might abuse the drug, depression, agitation, hypertension, or glaucoma. Ritalin™ requires a written prescription from a physician every 30 days.

Short-term effects that occur frequently but are not usually severe (and often disappear altogether after several days of usage) are as follows: appetite disturbances (not being hungry and/or some mild sense of stomach upset), sleep disturbances such as insomnia, rebound hyperactivity, and increased irritability or mood change.

Reported long-term effects are of greater concern to parents. At one time, children who took Ritalin™ were thought to be at risk for decreased growth. However, research has not substantiated any significant differences in growth curves between children on or off the medication when followed through adolescence. Nevertheless, most physicians monitor height and weight as well as obtain an annual CBC and chemical profile. The occurrence of motor tics (muscle twitches or abnormal motor movements) is of more serious concern. Any nervous tic that occurs in association with Ritalin™ should be reported to a physician immediately.

Symptoms of lethargy or depression are often the result of a dosage of the medication that is too high, the need for an alternative medication, or an incorrect diagnosis.

EXHIBIT 2.1 Medication Fact Sheet

Student——————————————————————— Date———————————————

Parent (Guardian) _____

Teacher——————————————————— School Nurse——————————————

Physician ———————————————————————————————————————

Current medication dosage ——————————————————————————————

Time administered at school ————————————————————————————

OBSERVATIONS:

Have you noticed or has the student complained of any of the following side effects? How often? When?

Decreased appetite _____

Insomnia ——————————————————————————————————————

Stomachaches ——————————————————————————————————

Headaches ———————————————————————————————————————

Prone to crying —————————————————————————————————————

Tics/nervous movements ——————————————————————————————

Dizziness_____

Drowsiness_____

Anxiety_____

Social withdrawal _____

Irritability_____

Sadness_____

Staring _____

Verbally abusive behavior_____

FORM 2.3 Medication Follow-Up Report

Have you noticed any fluctuations in behavior throughout the day? If so, describe. Describe the student's attentiveness (i.e., distractibility, listening, on-task behavior, and concentration).

Describe the student's impulse control (i.e., acting before thinking, shifting from one activity to another, supervision required, interrupting, awaiting turn).

Describe the student's physical activity level (i.e., ability to sit still or remain seated, always on the go).

CURRENT ACADEMIC LEVELS:

Excellent   Good   Fair   Poor

CURRENT PEER INTERACTIONS:

Excellent   Good   Fair   Poor

OTHER CONCERNS:

McEwan, E., & Damer, M. *Managing Unmanageable Students: Practical Solutions for Administrators.* © 2000, Corwin Press, Inc.

Adapted by permission of Kenosha Unified School District #1, Kenosha, Wisconsin. Readers may reproduce this document for their professional use,

FORM 2.3 Continued

- Provide teacher with student's medication schedule.

- Provide positive verbal praise.

- Assign the nurse to educate the student on the benefits of taking a particular medication.

- Have an adult or peer escort the student to the office for medication.

- Have the student wear a digital watch with an alarm as a reminder.

- Use a school/home reward system for complying with medication.

Keeping information flowing back and forth between school and medical professionals is also a key responsibility of the nurse.

The social worker also has a valuable role to play in the information-sharing process, that of interfacing with mental health professionals who may be seeing the student. For example, Ms. Brickert, the social worker, talked with Richard's counselor at the mental health center (after the parent had signed a release at the center authorizing such a conversation to take place), and discovered that the counselor had been working with Richard and his mother on a home behavior plan. With this knowledge, the school team was able to coordinate their plan with the counselor's plan to ensure Richard's success both at home and at school.

Medical and mental health professionals need to be regularly informed about what is happening at school. With information made available by school personnel, they can coordinate their plans with the interventions and strategies being implemented at school as well as offer support and reinforcement to parents (see Form 2.4, Authorization for Release/Exchange of Confidential Information, and Exhibit 2.2, Notification of Release of Confidential Information).

If the student with unmanageable behavior receives special education services, an important source of information is his or her special education files. The IEP probably lists instructional adaptations that were agreed on by the parents and school staff. Never assume that these adaptations are being consistently implemented in the classroom; misplaced paperwork and the high demands on teachers' time and energy often result in oversights. Although the absence of the prescribed instructional adaptations may not be associated with the student's current behavior, the frustration caused by neglect of the recommended adaptations can trigger disruptive behavior that could have been prevented. Parents who are aware that these adaptations to which they agreed are not taking place feel helpless when confronted with their child's disruptive behavior. Justifiably or not, they believe that if the teacher consistently carried out the adaptations, their child's behavior would not be an issue.

If Zachary, who moved into the district last year, is supposed to take all of his tests in the special education teacher's room because his reading level is several grades below that of the other students, and he further needs to have the test questions read aloud to him until his reading ability

Student: Name————————— Sex ————— Birth Date —————————

Address: ————————————————————————————————
(include number, street, city, state, and zip)

As the parent or legal guardian of the above named child, I hereby grant my permission to:
to exchange information with: (Include name and address).

————————————————————————————————————

————————————————————————————————————

Check those records to be released:

———— Functional Behavioral Analysis Documentation (e.g., Behavior Function Grid, On-Task Data, Behavior Intervention Plan)

———— Student Permanent Record
(Basic identifying information: academic transcript, attendance records, health records, honors or awards, school-sponsored activities)

———— Student Temporary Record
(Family background information, IQ scores, group and individual scores, psychological evaluations, achievement level test results, extracurricular activities, disciplinary information)

———— Special Education Records
(Reports of multidisciplinary staffings on which placement was based, all records and reports relating to special education placement, hearings and appeals)

———— Occupational/Physical Therapy Evaluation Reports

———— Psychological Evaluation Report and/or Diagnostic Test Scores

———— Social and Health History

———— Speech and Language Records and Reports

The purpose of this authorization is: ————————————————————

————————————————————————————————————
Signature of Parent or Guardian   Date
                                        (Valid for one year)

————————————————————————————————————
Signature of Student   Phone
(Age 12 and older)

                          ————————————————————————
                          Person Securing Consent

McEwan, E., & Damer, M. *Managing Unmanageable Students: Practical Solutions for Administrators.*
© 2000, Corwin Press, Inc.

Reprinted by permission of West Chicago Elementary District #33, West Chicago, IL. Readers may reproduce this document for their professional use.

FORM 2.4 Authorization for Release/Exchange of Confidential Information

January 1, 2002

Mr. and Mrs. James Markham
1221 Mona Lisa Dr.
Smalltown, IL 00000

Dear Mr. and Mrs. Markham:

As a follow-up to our recent meeting regarding Matthew and his behavioral difficulties at
school, information regarding the behavior intervention plan we developed was sent (as
per your written consent) to Dr. Stephen Deardorff, Matthew's psychologist, on
December 21, 2001. Please provide us with regular updates regarding your visits with Dr.
Deardorff. This can be done by calling the school psychologist, Ms. Susan Welby, at 555-
2431, by sending notes to Dr. Welby at school, or by instructing Dr. Deardorff to send
copies of his reports to Ms. Welby at 1221 Mona Lisa Dr., Smalltown, IL.

Thank you for following up with this most important matter in your child's education. We
look forward to working with you and your doctor to help Matthew maximize his school
experience.

Sincerely,

Donald Stephens, Principal
Smalltown Elementary School

McEwan, E., & Damer, M. *Managing Unmanageable Students: Practical Solutions for Administrators.*
© 2000, Corwin Press, Inc.

Reprinted by permission of West Chicago Elementary District #33, West Chicago, IL. Readers may adapt
this letter for their own professional use.

EXHIBIT 2.2 Notification of Release of Confidential Information

improves, then this adaptation should consistently occur. Aside from the legal obligation you have to follow IEP recommendations, you may also find that Zachary was sent to your office after he no longer could endure sitting at his desk for 20 minutes staring at the test he was unable to read. The test he could not read was the trigger that set off his behavior. Too many principals have assumed that their staff members are routinely following IEP adaptations for an unmanageable student only to find themselves in a due process hearing where the parent's attorneys present evidence to the contrary.

Grant was a student with Tourette syndrome whom the school district claimed was so disruptive that he should be transferred to a special, self-contained school for students with behavior disorders. Months later and under the tension of a due process hearing, the parents' attorney pointed out that Grant's disruptive behavior had been caused by a teacher who did not follow the IEP recommendations. The teacher was supposed to encourage Grant to go to the nurse's office to "cool off" when he needed to release the pent up tension that resulted from his efforts to hold in some of his vocal tics. Not only did the teacher fail to encourage Grant to "cool off," he even refused to let him leave the classroom when Grant recognized his need.

How can you ensure accountability and be certain that IEP mandated adaptations are taking place? It is up to you to set the tone for your school. If adaptations were agreed to in the IEP, then staff members need to know that they are expected to make them consistently. Just as it is not enough for many of your teachers to rely on their memory after reading student files at the beginning of the year, do not rely on your memory. Make a list of IEP adaptations for any students in your school who pose discipline problems and tack it up in your office where you routinely look. Make it a weekly habit to ask the teachers of IEP students if the adaptations they are using are working or, better yet, stop in and observe for yourself. Mark the date you observed the adaptation was being used on the IEP adaptations list. If you delegate some of this oversight to the special education director or psychologist, you will increase your monitoring capability. This effort will ensure that your staff consistently follows through on IEP adaptations and will engender trust from parents in the process.

Triage If Necessary

You will rarely encounter an unmanageable student with just one behavior problem. The problems generated by students with unmanageable behaviors may remind you of the havoc Pandora loosed upon the earth when she opened her box in the ancient myth. A triage prioritizing system similar to that used in a hospital emergency room should be employed. Determine which behavior problem is of the highest priority and start with that one problem. Discipline problems that are potentially harmful to the student or to other students or staff demand immediate action. Leaving the classroom, playground area, or school building or exhibiting physical aggression toward other students or staff members are obviously high-priority behaviors. All students and staff deserve a safe school environment, and your primary responsibility is to ensure the highest level of safety for everyone. Disrespectful or threatening language as well as disturbing others with hands, feet, and/or objects may also fall into the high-priority category if they are perceived as threatening by staff and other students.

After resolving high-priority behaviors, focus on medium-priority behaviors. These behaviors interfere with classroom instruction and the academic mission of your school. When a student disrupts the classroom or subverts the authority of school staff, other students' learning stops. The following are usually medium-priority behaviors:

- Use of disrespectful and/or threatening language

- Disturbing others with hands, feet, and/or objects

- Inappropriate use of school materials

- Talking out in class

- Being out of seat

- Noncompliance with teacher's requests and directions

A student's inability to work independently without adult intervention or the exhibition of nondisruptive, disorganized behaviors are typically considered low-priority behaviors that, although annoying to the teacher, do not directly interfere with the learning of other students. These behaviors do interfere with the learning of the student who engages in them, however, and you cannot afford to ignore them because they will usually trigger higher-priority behaviors. For example, a student in middle school who still cannot complete an independent school project might direct rude comments to the teacher to escape a frustrating work situation. A fourth-grade student who cannot complete a 15-minute writing assignment independently might leave his or her desk and fiddle with materials at another student's desk to escape the demands of the assignment.

Step 2: Where, When, and How Often
Is the Behavior Occurring?

The Importance of Data

If your teachers know that whenever they approach you about a student's behavior problem you will ask for specific details about the behavior and data related to how often the behavior is occurring, they will routinely begin to use the recommended data collection techniques. Very soon, data will be regarded as an indispensable tool to the problem-solving process rather than as the dreaded "D" word.

Your personal involvement in the data collection procedure is essential until your teachers become accustomed to analyzing their classrooms objectively as a part of resolving any serious behavior issue. Later, you can delegate data collection to other staff members who are part of the child's team. When you or any other observer use data rather than a narrative to communicate about behavior, you will more readily penetrate the wall of resistance a teacher can raise when asked to change his or her instruction or classroom management. A principal who tells a teacher that he or she is too punitive with a student will make more headway if the discussion begins with hard data. For example, "During the half-hour I was in your classroom, I noted that you praised the student zero times, whereas during that same time I counted 24 critical comments and corrections." The teacher cannot dismiss your observations as easily when you create a databased record of what was said. Concerns about instructional effectiveness or behavior are far more readily communicated through the objectivity of data.

Communications to parents that are grounded in solid data will be more readily accepted as well. A statement to parents that Wanda left her desk 10 times during language arts class and attempted to distract other students from their work will help the parents picture their student's disruptive behavior. Had the principal simply told the parents that their daughter was disrupting the class, they would have been more likely to dismiss the principal's concerns as unwarranted or judgmental toward their daughter.

Ideally you will collect data for several days before developing a resolution plan. If you are forced to react and move into immediate planning because the student's behavior has created an emergency situation, then you have no choice but to implement a plan and collect data simultaneously. Revise the plan if data collection uncovers new information.

The Cardinal Rules of Data Collection

Three basic rules govern successful data collection. Unless you follow them, data collection will be ineffective and your problem-solving process will break down.

1. Unless data collection is easy and interferes minimally with classroom routines, it will not be collected.

2. Unless the process is perfected through practice, it will appear cumbersome and data will not be collected.

3. Unless someone else will look at the data and review it with the person who has collected it, the data will not be collected.

Methods for Recording Data

We recommend two methods for recording data: (a) the Frequency Count Method, and (b) the Momentary Time Sampling Method. See Form 2.5, Guidelines for Selecting Data Recording Method, to help you decide which method is preferable for use with each of the 10 problem behaviors. With both methods, focus your observations to times of the school day when the teacher has reported that the student is most likely to exhibit the problem behavior (e.g., during math class or silent reading).

Frequency Count Method. The Frequency Count Method can only be used with behaviors that are "countable." A countable behavior has a distinct beginning and ending, only lasts for a few minutes, and does not occur so rapidly in succession that counting is difficult. In most situations, a teacher can easily use the frequency count method without assistance. If the behavior is a high-priority problem that could result in injury to the student or someone else, then every incidence of the behavior should be recorded. Lower-priority behaviors can be recorded at intermittent periods during which they are most likely to occur. Use Form 2.6, the Problem Behavior Recording Form, to record when and how often the problem behavior occurs.

Suggest that teachers put the recording form on a clipboard so they can easily move around the room while counting. When the student goes to music class or gym, the classroom teacher can then pass the clipboard to that teacher. Record the student's behavior immediately after it occurs; do not rely on memory. A teacher's tally based on recollection rarely matches the exact number of times that the behavior actually occurs.

Always ask the teacher or other individual (e.g., lunchroom supervisor) in charge of the activity you observed whether the student's behavior during the time you watched was typical of a representative day and circle Y (yes) or N (no) depending on the answer. If students are not accustomed to your routine presence in the classroom, you might observe abnormally good behavior. Your goal, however, is to observe student behavior that is representative of a typical day. If you have questions about the process, see Exhibit 2.3, a Problem Behavior Recording Form that has been completed by an observer in an actual classroom situation.

Momentary Time Sampling Method. Although the frequency method is easier to use, not all behaviors can be accurately assessed by counting them. When faced with assessing more complex, noncountable behaviors, sit in the classroom and collect time-sampling data on the problem behavior(s) for 10-minute periods on several different occasions. The following are four conditions under which to use the Momentary Time Sampling (MTS) Method:

1. If the student's problem behavior is not easily countable.

(text continues on page 36)

Use Frequency Data Collection Method for behaviors that are easily countable, have a definite start and stop, are not long-lasting, and that are roughly of equivalent duration.

Use Momentary Time Sampling Data Collection Method for behaviors with longer duration, that occur too frequently to count, that occur in rapid succession, or that do not have a definite start and stop.

Ten Problem Behaviors	Frequency Method	MTS Method
Leaving the classroom, playground area, or school building	Count each occurrence of this behavior.	--
Physical aggression toward others with hands, feet, and objects	Count each occurrence of this behavior.	--
Disturbing others with hands, feet, and/or objects	These behaviors are usually countable because of their distinct onset and stopping point.	If the student loudly pounds the desk for extended periods of time, or engages in a combination of these behaviors several times per minute, then use MTS to assess.
Inappropriate use of school materials	These behaviors are usually countable because of their distinct onset and stopping point and because they only last for several moments.	If the student engages in these behaviors so frequently that it is difficult to accurately count them, use MTS to assess.
Talking out in class	If the student typically talks out for short time periods (less than 2 or 3 minutes), count each occurrence.	If the student engages in longer conversation exchanges that often last more than a few minutes, use MTS to assess.
Out of seat	If the student typically leaves his or her seat or desk area for short time periods (less than 2 minutes), count each occurrence.	If the student leaves his or her desk for longer time periods, use MTS to assess.
Disrespectful and/or threatening language	Count each occurrence of the behavior.	--
Noncompliance with teacher's requests and directions	These behaviors are usually countable because of their distinct onset and stopping point.	If the student typically refuses to work by turning away from instruction or putting his head on the desk for longer periods of time, use MTS to assess.
Inability to work independently without adult intervention	- -	MTS is most accurate for taking data on a constellation of *off-* or *on-task* behaviors
Nondisruptive disorganized	- -	MTS is most accurate for taking data on a constellation of *off-* or *on-task* behaviors

McEwan, E., & Damer, M. *Managing Unmanageable Students: Practical Solutions for Administrators.* © 2000, Corwin Press, Inc.

FORM 2.5 Guidelines for Selecting Data Recording Method

Student:
Teacher:
Date:
Problem Behavior(s):

Mark the behavior in the second column each time it occurs. If you are keeping track of two behaviors, use the first letter of the behavior-name to indicate an occurrence (e.g., write a "t" each time a "Talkout" occurs and an "i" for "Inappropriate Use of School Materials").

	Tally	Notes
Start Time: Stop Time: Class: Activity: Representative: Y N		
Start Time: Stop Time: Class: Activity: Representative: Y N		
Start Time: Stop Time: Class: Activity: Representative: Y N		
Start Time: Stop Time: Class: Activity: Representative: Y N		

FORM 2.6 Problem Behavior Recording Form

Student: **Darcy Matthews**
Teacher: **Martha Holmes**
Date:**1/04**
Problem Behavior(s): **Inappropriate use of school materials**

Mark the behavior in the second column each time it occurs. If you are keeping track of two behaviors, use the first letter of the behavior-name to indicate an occurrence (e.g., write a "t" each time a "Talkout" occurs and an "i" for "Inappropriate Use of School Materials").

	TALLY	NOTES
Start Time: **8:40** Stop Time: **9:10** Class: **Math** Activity: **Manipulatives** Representative: (Y) N	‖‖‖ ‖‖‖ ‖‖ **13**	**Blocks seemed distracting. Unless I was nearby, she stacked and pushed over.**
Start Time: **9:20** Stop Time: **9:50** Class: **Gym** Activity: **Dodgeball** Representative: (Y) N	‖ **1**	**Appeared to be interested in game. Played with enthusiasm.**
Start Time: **10:00** Stop Time: **10:40** Class: **Language Arts** Activity: **Reading book, journal writing** Representative (Y) N	‖‖‖‖ **5**	**During journal writing, she karate-chopped a pencil.**
Start Time: **10:40** Stop Time: **11:00** Class: **Science** Activity: **Racing cars we had made the day before; recording speeds** Representative: Y (N)	‖‖‖‖ ‖‖‖‖ **10**	**Darcy was racing her car over other students' desks and up the classroom walls.**

McEwan, E., & Damer, M. *Managing Unmanageable Students: Practical Solutions for Administrators.*
© 2000, Corwin Press, Inc.

EXHIBIT 2.3   Completed Problem Behavior Recording Form

2. If you cannot tell when one incident begins or ends.

3. If the behavior lasts longer than 4 or 5 minutes.

4. If the behavior occurs rapidly in succession.

Teachers will be unable to teach and collect MTS data at the same time. Enlist data taking assistance from classroom aides, special education teachers, the social worker, or the school psychologist.

To ensure that your staff members understand the need for and know how to collect a momentary time sample, conduct a short in-service to teach this skill. Practice either in real classroom situations or while watching a videotape of one of your classrooms. School staff members are usually hesitant the first few times that they use the MTS method. For example, a novice data taker may be unsure whether the decision to mark on-task behavior for the student who was looking at his workbook instead of at the teacher was the correct decision. To eliminate this insecurity, have the novice practice taking data with another person two or three times and then compare the two sets of data. Each pair of data takers should practice until they get at least 80% agreement with their data. This type of practice session provides the novice with reassurance that his or her decisions parallel those of a partner.

Use Form 2.7, the Momentary Time Sampling Data Form, and a digital watch. Sitting to the side of the classroom, watch the student and record a "+" if the target behavior occurred at the exact instant the interval ends. If the behavior does not occur at the exact instant the interval ends, record a "-" mark. If the student displays the behavior during the middle of the interval, but stops before the exact instant the interval ends, rely on the accuracy of this sampling method and record a nonoccurrence of the behavior. Keep your eyes shifting between the moving digital display of seconds and the student whom you are watching. The very instant the digital display changes to 10 seconds, mark whether the student is displaying the behavior. When the digital display next changes to 20 seconds, mark whether the student displayed the behavior at that next instant. As each 10-second interval ends, move across the page to the right, eventually moving down the columns with the passage of each minute.

Once you have collected 10 minutes of data and completed the form, scan the completed data sheet and count the number of intervals in which you recorded the behavior as occurring (each box = one interval). Divide this number by the total number of intervals in which the behavior occurred and multiply by 100 to obtain the percent of occurrence. Time sampling data collected over several 10-minute periods during different activities and in different classes will provide an accurate estimate of the percentage of intervals that Caitlin is typically on-task or the percentage of intervals that Jamal roams the classroom.

As with frequency recording, ask the person in charge of the activity you were observing whether the student's behavior during the time you

Student: _____

Date: _____

Teacher: _____

Setting: _____

Activity: _____

Behavior: _____

Start Time: _____ Stop Time: _____

Key: + Behavior occurred at the **end** of the interval.

      - Behavior did **not** occur at the end of the interval.

Minutes	10"	20"	30"	40"	50"	60"
1						
2						
3						
4						
5						
6						
7						
8						
9						
10						

<u>Number of intervals where behavior occurred</u> x 100 = percent of occurrence
           Total Number of Intervals

_____ x 100 = _____ percent of occurrence

Representative: Y N

McEwan, E., & Damer, M. *Managing Unmanageable Students: Practical Solutions for Administrators.*
© 2000, Corwin Press, Inc.

FORM 2.7 Momentary Time Sampling Data Form

watched was typical of a representative day and circle Y (yes) or N (no). Your goal is to observe truly representative student behavior.

For confirmation that you have completed the process correctly, compare your completed recording sheet to Exhibit 2.4, a sample Momentary Time Sampling Data Form that has been completed by an observer in an actual classroom.

Step 3: What Do the Parents and the Student Think?

In working to resolve the problems posed by an unmanageable student, interview the parents to obtain the information needed to complete the Motivation Analysis Form, Form 2.8. The questions on the form are similar to those used by managers in resolving problems with employees. Managers recognize that when they want to change the behavior of employees (e.g., get them to come to work on time or complete their work with a higher accuracy rate), they are more likely to have success if they know what makes the problem employees tick. Although a principal will typically have limited influence on the dynamics in a student's home setting, he or she will nevertheless need to know some details about how the student operates in that context. Who are the student's friends? What do the parents see as the student's greatest strengths and weaknesses in the home environment? What does the student reveal about the frustrations or joys of school at the end of the day? We cannot hope to resolve a discipline problem if we do not know the answers to these questions.

Not only will you obtain valuable insight from parents' answers, you will have taken an important first step in including them as part of your team. Although the parents of an unmanageable student will often initially fail to admit that their child poses serious problems in the home setting, during a nonthreatening conversation they may begin to share incidents of similar problems at home. When parents see that someone from the school shows an interest in understanding their child's interests and strengths as well as difficulties, they are far more likely to work with the school in partnership to resolve the problem. If the parents of an unmanageable child are capable of supporting a behavior intervention at home, such as only allowing video games on nights when no rude language has occurred during the school day, you are well on your way toward working cooperatively. If the parents are incapable of following through at home or unwilling to support the plan, then at least you have established a respectful, positive relationship with the parents. Hopefully, they will appreciate the energy and planning that are taking place to resolve their child's behavior problems at school.

Information that you glean from working with the parents to complete the motivational form can provide unexpected clues for resolving the student's unmanageable behavior. You may be unaware that Maria recently began taking asthma medicine, which could explain some of the

Student: **Terrence**
Date: **10/12/98**
Setting: **Fifth Grade Math Class**
Activity: **Large Group Discussion**
Behavior: **On-task**
Start Time: **10:40**
Stop Time: **10:50**

Key: + Behavior occurred at the <u>end</u> of the interval.
     - Behavior did <u>not</u> occur at the end of the interval.

Minutes	10"	20"	30"	40"	50"	60"
1	+	-	+	-	+	+
2	-	-	-	-	+	+
3	+	+	+	+	+	+
4	+	+	+	+	+	+
5	+	-	-	-	-	-
6	-	+	-	+	+	+
7	+	+	+	+	-	+
8	+	-	+	-	+	+
9	+	+	-	-	-	+
10	+	-	+	-	-	-

<u>Number of intervals where behavior occurred</u> x 100 = percent of occurrence
        Total Number of Intervals

37/60 x 100 = 62% percent of occurrence: On-task

Representative: (Y) N

McEwan, E., & Damer, M. *Managing Unmanageable Students: Practical Solutions for Administrators.* © 2000, Corwin Press, Inc.

EXHIBIT 2.4 Completed Momentary Time Sampling Data Form

Date: _____

Student Name: _____   Teacher: _____

1. What is the student's attitude toward school?

2. What events or situations make the student angry or frustrated?

3. What events or situations make the student happy or motivate him or her?

4. What are the student's major strengths?

5. What are the student's major weaknesses?

6. Does the student have any friends at school? In the community?

7. What are some of the things the student worries about—problems in and out of
    school?

8. What is the student's greatest ambition or goal?

9. What are the student's outside interests and hobbies?

10. Describe the student's health. Has his or her health changed in any way in the past 6
    months?

11. Is the student taking any medication? What are the side effects of the medication?

McEwan, E., & Damer, M. *Managing Unmanageable Students: Practical Solutions for Administrators.*
© 2000, Corwin Press, Inc.

FORM 2.8 Motivation Analysis Form

recent off-task behaviors she has been displaying in the mornings. Cameron's parents may not have informed the school that 2 weeks ago the doctor prescribed Ritalin™, which although taken at home, could have triggered those playground fights.

Sometimes parents have found solutions for unmanageable behaviors that will transfer to the school. Jennifer's love of cartoon drawing could give the teacher an idea to reward her with drawing opportunities for appropriate classroom behavior. A father's suggestion that 5 minutes of jogging helps Tom blow off steam when he becomes unduly frustrated at home might give you an idea of how to prevent his frequent trips to your office.

Step 4: What Patterns Emerge From Examining the Data?

Looking for Patterns

Collecting observation data on a student provides the information that is needed to elucidate patterns associated with a problem behavior. An astute observer will always jot down notes about what happened just before the problem behavior occurred and what came after. The challenge is twofold: to recognize environmental factors that appear to trigger the behavior and to gain a sense of how the adults and students in the classroom typically react to the behavior. They may (a) encourage the disruptive behavior by laughing at it or giving it undue attention, (b) react to the disruptive behavior with disapproval or punishments, or (c) ignore the behavior. Ignoring is always regarded as a specific consequence.

As you sit in a classroom and record a mark every time Richard throws paper or leaves his seat, ask yourself what happened just before he displayed each of those behaviors and what was the reaction of the teacher and students immediately following them. If you ask these specific questions you may be more apt to recognize that every time the teacher gave Richard a writing task, Richard displayed disruptive behavior. The fine motor requirements of writing tasks could have been so frustrating that they provided the trigger. You might also observe that the teacher ignored Richard's behavior half of the time, criticized him at other times, and once stroked his arm gently to encourage him to move back to his desk. The teacher might have unknowingly precipitated an increase in the disruptive behavior by inconsistently following her class rules. These are important clues to consider when developing a plan to resolve the problems caused by Richard's disruptive behavior.

Use Form 2.9, the Before-and-After Form, to record what happens just before and just after the disruptive behavior. Looking at a sequence of events related to the disruptive behavior will highlight patterns that might otherwise be missed. Sometimes the action that a teacher takes just after the disruptive behavior becomes the trigger for the next occurrence.

Student:_____

Date: _____

Teacher: _____

Setting: _____

Activity: _____

Start Time:_____

Stop Time:_____

What Happened Before	Disruptive Behavior	What Happened After

McEwan, E., & Damer, M. *Managing Unmanageable Students: Practical Solutions for Administrators.*
© 2000, Corwin Press, Inc.

FORM 2.9 Before-and-After Form

What Happened Before?	Disruptive Behavior	What Happened After?
Peer student says target student never has homework.	Target student says, "Shut up!"	Teacher puts check on board.

EXHIBIT 2.5   Pattern 1

What Happened Before?	Disruptive Behavior	What Happened After?
Teacher puts check on board.	Target student says, "I hate this class!"	Teacher ignores student.

EXHIBIT 2.6   Pattern 2

Exhibits 2.5 and 2.6 illustrate what happened when a teacher's reaction became the trigger.

Following is a brief description of the observation that generated the exhibits:

> During a discussion of wellness during science, the student under observation shouts out "Shut up" to another student who tells him that he never has his homework done. The teacher puts a check mark on the board in response to the rude language of the observed student, after which the student stands up and says, "I hate this class." Hearing this, the teacher walks away and asks the class a question about the assignment.

What Comes Next?

Many administrators and building teams rush to solve behavior problems without an adequate database. If you have carefully followed Steps 1 through 4, you have the "information advantage": details about the student, his home, and what specific situations and events trigger his behavior. You are now ready to tackle Steps 5 through 10, in which you will put the finishing touches on the Functional Behavioral Assessment your team has been compiling and move on to design a Behavior Intervention Plan. Chapter 3 will provide the information and tools you need to complete that task.

CHAPTER THREE

What You Need to Do

Wouldn't it be wonderful if we never had to solve any of our students' behavior problems? We could sit around with our teams and endlessly speculate about causes, patterns, and possibilities. We could hypothesize and pontificate forever. You will have a certain number of team members who would like to just keep talking. They do not want to make decisions or come to conclusions. You do, however, live in the real world, and even if you and your staff members never completely uncover or discover all there is to know about a student, there comes a point at which you must just do it. Now that you and your staff have made the necessary observations, collected the pertinent data, and solicited parental input (Steps 1 through 4), you are nearly ready to create a workable plan.

The Principal's List

Before you schedule that planning meeting, however, there are several important things that you, the building principal, must think about and do. The development and implementation of a successful plan depends on your total involvement and commitment. You cannot ask more of your staff than you are willing to contribute.

Things to Do

Assemble the Planning Team

The classroom teachers who actually work with the student, those individuals who will be responsible for making the adaptations and implementing the plan, must always be a part of developing it. Never ask a teacher to implement a plan into which he or she had no input. Teachers who have worked successfully with the student in the past, or teachers who generally work well with difficult students might also be considered as team members. You may also wish to add support staff members to the team. Determine if the psychologist, social worker, special education staff, or any other support staff might have helpful expertise that will help with planning and be sure to include them. If the student takes medication or is seeing a counselor, psychologist, or psychiatrist, the school nurse will be a key member of the planning team.

Decide Whether to Involve the Parents

Some principals always involve parents in the initial planning meeting. Others either talk to them by phone or have a mini-meeting a few days later with the understanding that modifications will be made depending on their input into the plan. Consider the following questions when deciding how to involve parents:

1. Are the parents willing to work in a team effectively? Do they have an adversarial relationship with the school?

2. Does the child have an IEP and do the parents request direct involvement in every step of the planning process?

3. Have your staff members learned to deal with controversy assertively rather than aggressively?

4. Is this a first-time team meeting regarding the student or have you tried several approaches without success? Is your team beginning to consider a change of placement?

Things to Think About

Think About Your Role as a Change Agent

In addition to determining who will attend the meeting and how they will be involved, there are several important leadership roles to think about. Although some principals delegate the responsibility of attending the team planning meeting to their assistants, special education directors, or a consulting behavior consultant, the principal who takes personal responsibility for these sometimes volatile meetings is more assured of success because of *E-Quation*.

E-Quation is a term we have coined to describe the fact that an individual's motivation to put forth effort and energy toward the solution of a problem increases in direct proportion to the hands-on involvement of that individual's evaluator. Because of the variety of positions that both of the authors have held over the years, we have come to realize the practical benefits of E-Quation when working with adults who were hesitant to make needed changes. Just as the presence of a teacher notches up the performance of off-task students, your presence in team meetings will act as a positive extrinsic motivator for staff members who might prefer to hand off a student's behavior problem to someone else. When the principal is added to the problem-solving equation, all of the participants will be more creative, energetic, and motivated.

Think About Your Role in Resolving Controversy

If you typically assume the role of facilitator in team meetings, merely sitting on the sidelines and assisting the group, be prepared to assume a more active role if your staff has little experience developing behavior intervention plans. You may be required to resolve an impasse if the group becomes locked in disagreement over what interventions to select. If the teacher is opposed to trying an instructional adaptation, the conversation turns unprofessionally negative about the parents, or the lunchroom needs more supervision during the student's most difficult time of day, your leadership is needed. Because each staff member comes to the table with his or her own ideas about behavior as well as with personality styles that range from rigid to flexible, you can expect heated discussions and conflict during team meetings. Not only will group members disagree about the function of the student's behavior, but also about possible methods of resolution. Remember that conflict among team members is natural and even productive as you help to move the team from disagreement to workable solutions.

Think for a moment about the diverse ideas your staff members have in a typical planning meeting as you develop an action plan for Jeremy, a middle school student who frequently fails to follow his teachers' directions, complete in-class assignments, or do homework. In addition to his pervasive refusals to work, Jeremy has made verbal threats to students and staff on a number of occasions, been physically aggressive to another student on two occasions, and periodically made audible rude comments under his breath to teachers.

The social worker attending the meeting might believe that until Jeremy has made more progress in his counseling sessions, no significant changes will occur. The psychologist might repeatedly bring the discussion back to Jeremy's reading deficits, whereas Jeremy's English teacher, with whom he has the most trouble, sits in stony silence. A special education teacher you invited might suggest trying a motivation system of awarding points every hour for listening to the teacher and eliminating verbal or physical aggression. Jeremy's history teacher might insist that the police be called the next time any verbal aggression occurs. She believes that only decisive, punitive discipline has any chance of resolving Jeremy's problems.

This stalemate provides a perfect opportunity to apply the team leadership skills you have acquired. Until your team is more experienced and has some success at developing action plans that bring results, you must serve as the guide and decision maker when resolution appears hopeless. Otherwise, you could be sitting in that room trying to develop a plan until the semester ends. Once you have listened to each person's perspective and supporting rationale, ask probing questions, ensure that school rules and legal restrictions are followed, and help shape a detailed plan of action that can be implemented within the next few days. If your staff members cannot come to agreement on a plan, you must prioritize for them, assertively deciding which course of action the team will try first. Remind team members that other proposed actions can be tried later if the first plan is not successful.

Think About Your Role in Delegating

If your staff is unaccustomed to developing action plans for unmanageable students that are similar to our model, expect that the initial team meetings will take more time. As your staff becomes accustomed to the process they will easily develop action plans within an hour. To help everyone stay on-task during the team meeting and to ensure that you do not neglect any part of the process, complete each item on the Behavior Intervention Planning Form, Form 2.1. Some principals choose to delegate team gatekeeping functions such as identifying when team members are off-task and redirecting them. Other principals assume those gatekeeping functions themselves.

Decide before the team meeting who will act as a gatekeeper and determine who will keep detailed notes. To ensure that you have the documentation required by the new IDEA for a student's Functional Behavioral Assessment, always have the assigned note taker complete the Functional Behavioral Assessment Documentation Form (Form 3.1) as your team defines, identifies, and analyzes the problem(s). This documentation form that parallels the Behavior Intervention Planning Form (Form 2.1) can be easily transferred into a student's IEP. Because each team member can walk away from a planning meeting with a different idea about the team's decision, we suggest providing an outline of the final plan to all participants to minimize misunderstanding.

Think About Your Role in Allocating Resources

Often, the action plan that is developed requires resources or changes that only you can facilitate. If the team recommends sending the unmanageable student to the nurse's office for a 5-minute cool down to prevent an explosion during a tough history class, you will need to make arrangements with the nurse. In one school, a creative team decided to reward an unmanageable student with two extra gym periods per week if he was compliant with the teacher and kept his hands and feet to himself when

(text continues on page 51)

Student: _____ Teacher(s): _____

Person Completing Form: _____

Use the Behavior Intervention Planning Form, Form 2.1, to log in completion dates. Forms 2.1 and 3.1 are parallel forms with corresponding items and numbers/letters.

1a. Describe undesirable target behavior(s) to decrease and determine whether of high, medium, or low priority.

        <u>Undesirable Target Behavior(s)</u>   <u>Priority Level</u>

1b. Describe desirable target behavior(s) to increase.

1c. List or attach a copy of classroom rules that teacher has established.

1d. List interventions that staff members have already tried.

McEwan, E., & Damer, M. *Managing Unmanageable Students: Practical Solutions for Administrators.* © 2000, Corwin Press, Inc.

FORM 3.1 Functional Behavioral Assessment Documentation Form

1e. List times of day when the problem is occurring most frequently.

Time of Day	Subject or Activity	Teacher

_____1f. Attach student interview notes. (optional)

_____1g. List any medications that student takes and attach fact sheet(s) about side effects. (if applicable)

2.a. - c. List relevant data and attach all data forms including on-task data (Form 2.7), reinforcement data (Form 4.1), and any other MTS or event data (Forms 2.6 and 2.7).

DATE	TYPE OF DATA	ACTIVITY/TEACHER	RESULTS

_____2d. Attach the completed Motivation Analysis Form (Form 2.8).
_____2e. Attach all completed "Before-and-After" data forms (Form 2.9).
_____2f. Attach any Medication Follow-Up Reports (Form 2.3) that have been completed. (if applicable)

FORM 3.1 Continued

3a. List curriculum demands and environmental factors that could be triggering the target disruptive behavior(s).

3b. List teacher behaviors that could be triggering or maintaining the target disruptive behavior(s).

3c. List frequent patterns that the team has identified with the target disruptive behaviors.

_____3d. Attach the completed Behavior Function Grid (Form 3.2).

Date Completed: _____

Signatures of participants:

_____   _____

_____   _____

_____   _____

McEwan, E., & Damer, M. *Managing Unmanageable Students: Practical Solutions for Administrators.* © 2000, Corwin Press, Inc.

FORM 3.1 Continued

he was with other students. Without the support of the school principal who asked the physical education teacher to make the change, this successful intervention would never have occurred.

On some occasions the action plan will recommend a desk partition in order to make a quiet workplace for a student or to provide an extra computer station in the classroom to use as a reward. Teachers are dependent on your budget juggling to make those extra materials available. If the playground needs more intensive supervision to prevent other students from taunting the unmanageable child, a situation that will predictably trigger his aggression, only you can creatively explore ways to reassign an additional person to the morning recess duty roster.

We hope that you are not daunted by the variety of roles you will play in helping your staff to develop a plan. Fine-tune your skills to facilitate and lead meetings such as these through practice and watching others who are more skilled. You will soon realize enormous personal and professional benefits. You will become more respected as a leader in your school and more influential in every aspect of school life. Staff, students, and parents will appreciate not only your educational expertise but also your caring and compassion. You will be trusted, not because you always give everyone exactly what they want, but because you listen and understand. Finally, you will grow emotionally and psychologically as you gain confidence to deal with your own personal fears of ineptitude and failure. The most important discovery you will make is that the power to promote change in staff, students, and parents comes only through self-understanding and self-management. As we noted at the outset: "If you want to change the behavior of others, change your own."

Once you have checked these items off your "to do" and "to think about" lists, you are ready to move through Steps 5 through 10.

The Problem-Solving Process: Steps 5 Through 10

Step 5: Figure Out What Needs to Change: Environmental, Instructional, and Curricular Adaptations

When a team convenes to analyze the classroom environment, instruction, and curriculum experienced by the unmanageable student, almost anyone at the table can feel threatened, but the student's teacher is especially vulnerable. After all, the team is putting the status quo under the microscope. Ineffective teaching behaviors often contribute to the unmanageable student's problem. The class in question may typically be on task only 50% of the time, as shown by the data the school psychologist gathered during 3 days last week. The teacher under scrutiny may have only one style of feedback to the unmanageable student—criticism. Unless instructional adaptations are made, any plan your team develops is doomed from the start.

Before you can determine what dynamics need to change, your team has to ask tough questions. How does the teacher respond when the student tells him that he forgot his homework? Are classroom rules consistently followed? What is the science teacher doing differently from everyone else that seems to explain why she never has any problems with the student? These questions are downright frightening for many teachers, especially if they have not previously participated in this process.

To determine what adaptations are likely to resolve the problems presented by the unmanageable student, minimize the intimidation factor for your staff. By relying on data and observation notes as the basis for describing the student's school environment and instruction, you can avoid judgmental language. Rather than asking Mr. Maltheny why he ignores the student unless misbehavior occurs, you can pull out your "Before-and-After" chart and descriptively relate a series of occurrences in the classroom as shown in this example:

This pattern on Friday appeared to be typical of what I see whenever Shawna is in math class. Let's look at what was happening. She came in the room like gangbusters, grabbing Alex's notebook away from him, an incident that you very patiently handled by reminding her that she needed to start working on the problem on the board. The next time the two of you connected was 20 minutes later when Shawna turned around and drew a heart on Matthew's paper. As soon as Matthew shrieked, you warned her that next time she would have to go to the office. I was pleased to see that she listened to you and got back to work for another 15 minutes. Five minutes into the cooperative group activity, however, you scolded her because she was trying to step on the toes of the student sitting next to her. When I look at all of the observation notes, I see a pattern in which almost all of your interactions with Shawna involve you catching and correcting her misbehavior.

The questions on the Behavior Intervention Planning Form (Form 2.1) under the heading "Analyze Problem," are some of the toughest ones you will ever discuss with your staff. We can assure you from personal experience, however, that as long as you maintain empathy, keep your observations nonjudgmental, and throw in a bit of humor now and then, you will lead your staff to improved instructional effectiveness. An aura of accountability will develop when teachers become accustomed to their teaching performance being microanalyzed. Excellent teachers are able to engage in metacognition regarding their teaching. At the end of lessons they ask themselves what worked and what did not work. They then alter their teaching based on that process of repeated examination. By sharing objective, data-based observations, you will help all of your teachers engage in this type of reflective behavior. A teacher who is caught in a "criticism trap" with students will suddenly become conscious about his or her criticism rate when shown a script of his or her comments. Another teacher who has been oblivious to the amount of wasted time in his or her classroom will realize in a flash when presented with the data that he or she is spending far too much time on transitions. Teachers who can successfully engage in self-examination and survive will become more effective teachers.

To maintain a nonjudgmental tone, begin the team meeting with a discussion of the data that you have collected (e.g., the observations made as part of the "Observe Problem" section of the Behavior Intervention Planning Form). Next, ask your team to answer the first three questions under the "Analyze Problem" section.

1. What curriculum demands and environmental factors could be triggering the target disruptive behavior(s)?

2. What teacher behaviors could be triggering or maintaining the target disruptive behavior(s)?

3. What are the frequent patterns associated with the target disruptive behaviors?

Because you are treading on sensitive territory with your staff as you analyze how both their teaching behaviors and the school curriculum might be affecting a given student, remain as objective and analytical as you can. Use the following model as you present your findings to the group:

1. First, explain the type of data you took and the time during which it was taken. For example, "Last Friday between 12:00 and 12:30, I observed Conrad during a math lesson and took some frequency data on how many times he talked out."

2. Remember to mention if the time period you observed was representative of a typical class according to the teacher.

3. Always begin talking about the data/observation by sharing an objective positive observation or an empathetic icebreaker. For example, "Ms. Greg, I noticed that you were very patient while the students were in groups. Nicole was trying her hardest to get your attention and you followed through with your resolve to ignore her for a few days in order to see if that would help. That must have been very difficult."

4. Focus the conversation on what you have objectively seen, for example, "After the students took out their books, this is what I saw." Avoid giving "why's" and "should's" when you describe the observation.

5. After each person talks about his or her data or observation, ask the student's teacher if he or she sees any patterns in the data. For example, "Do you notice anything in the data or observations that wasn't obvious while you were teaching the lesson?"

6. If the teacher does not recognize patterns or triggers to the student's off-task or disruptive behavior, present your observations in a nonevaluative manner. For example, "When I look at the observations from last week, I notice that although you are alert and consistently remind Sean to start working, he was only complimented once during all of the observations, when he volunteered and named the continents."

7. Be sure to mention all of the actions of the teacher that appeared to help the student. For example, "I noticed that you have Gyda sitting right in the front of class so you can help her get her materials organized before each class. Those reminders you gave during the transitions seemed to help her start the class prepared to work."

8. Assist the team in setting concrete goals for desired changes in instruction, indicating whether an action of the teacher should be increased, decreased, or started. For example, "I noticed that when you teach you only walk between your desk and the front row. I'd like to see if walking near Marc's row more frequently might help him stay on-task. Why don't we discuss whether increasing the active monitoring you are currently doing should be one of our instructional adaptations. What does everyone think?"

Step 6: Develop a Hypothesis About the Function/Purpose of the Behavior

If team members observing the student can determine the function that the disruptive behavior serves, they will uncover valuable clues to resolving the problem. If Ricardo is crumpling his worksheet papers into basketballs and slamming them into the wastebasket in the middle of class, he could be causing this disruption because he lacks the handwriting skills needed to generate an essay. Ricardo's disruptive behavior provides an "escape" function from a task he is unable to do. Eliminating Ricardo's disruptive behavior will not occur until someone teaches him to type or to write more legibly and fluently.

If Tory is dancing in the aisles of class, she might be seeking the attention of her peers. Her disruptive behavior functions to provide additional peer attention. The educator who wants to redirect Tory's theatrical performances might suggest that she sign up for the school play or join a group of students who help the kindergarten teacher during lunch recess. Such activities would provide more appropriate attention from peers.

Determining the function of a student's disruptive behavior can arouse heated debates among your staff members; each person's analysis will be closely tied to his or her area of expertise and view of human behavior. Educators who are behaviorists typically focus on the function of a student's behavior as either avoidance from task or attention from peers or adults. A speech pathologist usually looks for an inability to communicate interactive functions such as frustration, protest, or affection behind the behavior. An occupational therapist looks for neurological causal factors, noticing that the student's aggression occurs whenever the room is too hot. The school psychologist might look to explain the function of the student's behavior as motivated by a desire for power or revenge. Your role as principal is to help team members to sort through these diverse perspectives, drawing from each to develop a hypothesis about the function that the student's behavior serves. If your team's hypothesis accurately identifies the function of the behavior, the resulting plan that takes the function into account will more likely be effective. Many times you will find that a student's misbehavior is maintained by more than one function.

To make your task easier when you reach this step, we have developed a Behavior Function Grid (Form 3.2) listing common functions of student misbehavior. The horizontal axis names the 10 top behavior problems of students that we identified in Chapter 1. Listed down the vertical axis are 12 functions of misbehavior that we have commonly observed in our own experience. They reflect a variety of theoretical positions. In order to match functions with misbehavior, team members must ask, "What do we believe is maintaining the misbehavior? What purpose does the misbehavior appear to serve and why would the student continue to do it?"

The Functions of Behavior

The following descriptions of each function on the grid will help your team develop their hypothesis.

Seek attention from peers/adults. Some students misbehave to gain positive or negative attention from adults and/or peers. The laughter of classmates will only fuel their clowning behavior because negative attention is preferable to anonymity. Instead of feeling embarrassment when their name is called out after they break a rule, these students are more likely to repeat the same action. Lectures from the principal can be especially gratifying because they signify an added level of attention. Calling in the parent of an attention-seeking student for a conference may backfire if the student desires the additional flurry of attention.

Seek tangible reinforcement. Sue covets a pair of Doc Martens and steals a pair in the locker room. Blake wants a student's glitter pen and bullies

FUNCTION	BEHAVIOR	Leaving school grounds	Physical aggression	Disturbing others with hands, feet, objects	Disrespectful and/or threatening language	Inappropriate use of school materials	Talking out in class	Out of seat	Noncompliance	Inability to work independently	Disorganized behaviors			
Seek attention from peers and adults														
Seek tangible reinforcement														
Seek power over others														
Seek revenge														
Seek stimulation														
Avoid uncomfortable sensory stimulation														
Avoid fear														
Avoid guilt														
Need sleep, food, drink, or exercise														
Lack of social/academic skills														
Tics/Obsessive-compulsive behaviors														
Substance abuse														

Student: _____   Date: _____   Teacher: _____

him to get it. Mike wants money to buy snacks after school and harasses his teachers until they finally agree to pay him 50¢ for each class period in which he maintains order in their classrooms. These students misbehave to obtain concrete objects that they want.

Seek power over others. Some students' actions are propelled by the desire for power. Whether their desire to control the environment and the people in it stems from a feeling of helplessness or because they are accustomed to running the show, these students resent adult authority in their drive to be at the top of any pecking order. In their quest to dominate peers, the underlying theme becomes "to win is to control." A small group of these students will respond to routine teacher directions with a "no," expressing defiance to assert their power.

Seek revenge. Students seek revenge when they strike out at other students or the teacher to get even. Whether the injustice is imagined or real, these students are driven to retaliate. When bullying is rampant, staff members will also have to deal with the resultant misbehavior of those who have been bullied. A student may seek revenge at school for abuse or injustice at home. If a father bullies his son, that son may later walk into class hell-bent on getting revenge against his second period male teacher. The two students who went on a rampage in Littleton, Colorado, demonstrated the explosive potential of revenge.

Seek stimulation. Some students misbehave to receive needed sensory stimulation. Students who are bored in the classroom may need the stimulation that comes from challenging instructional material. When challenge does not come from academic learning material, these students look for it in other, less appropriate ways. Other students, referred to as "sensory seekers" by occupational therapists, unconsciously provide themselves with certain types of intense physical sensory experiences that they need. A student in the hallway vigorously pushing off his arms from wall-to-wall may need more sensory input to his joints and muscles. Another student may routinely chew on her clothes or pound fists on the desk to receive extra sensory input to her mouth and hands. A child with autism may flap his hands in front of his eyes to provide more visual stimulation.

Avoid uncomfortable sensory stimulation. Some students misbehave because they are oversensitive to sensory stimulation that would typically be considered nonirritating to other students. Loud noise levels, crowded hallways, and overheated rooms can trigger a "fight or flight" reaction in these students. The discomfort they experience propels them into either lashing out in anger or trying to flee the uncomfortable situation. A student who is unable to tolerate the jostling in the small hallway area where students wait in the morning, may suddenly explode (fight reaction) and push the students who are standing too close to her. A kindergartener may tantrum (fight reaction) rather than put her fingers into the squooshy fingerpaint. If the glaring lights and deafening noise in the lunchroom are intolerable for a student's sensory level, he may misbehave in order to be rewarded by eating in the secluded office (flight reaction) where students who throw food are sent.

Avoid fear. Some students feel a generalized fear at being in class. The trigger may be a variety of things: fear of being away from parents, being evaluated, becoming separated from the comforts and security of home, perhaps even learning itself. Their misbehavior is an effort to disrupt and stop the situation causing the fear.

Avoid guilt. Some students bring a load of guilt to class for any of a variety of personal reasons. If they believe that they are "bad," they may try to make everyone else in the class "bad" to camouflage their own guilt. They may think, "I have bullied kids and stolen, but I'm not so bad because everyone else is also bad." Or they may try to subvert the moral authority of the teacher so that he or she is not in a position to make any valid moral judgments altogether. "You think I'm bad, but you're worse." Clowning may be a way of further disrupting moral authority by showing that "everything is a joke."

Need sleep, food, drink, or exercise. Some students whose misbehavior is triggered by the need for sleep, food, or drink may have an underlying medical problem. Others may come from households where food is in short supply or where bedtime and nutritious mealtime routines are not maintained. By fourth period class, Tatiana's hunger resulted in high levels of irritability that she usually displayed by verbally fighting with other students, calling them names and swearing like characters in a "South Park" episode. Her metabolism and blood sugar levels required more frequent and smaller meals throughout the day to avoid late morning explosions. Downstairs in another class, Ken was listless to the point of noncompliance from a lack of food. After his dad was laid off, Ken's family had to skip meals to provide shelter. Interruptions of sleep such as nightmares or apnea, difficulty going to sleep, hypoglycemia, and diabetes are some other triggers causing a student to need food, sleep, or drink. High energy students may need more opportunities to exercise during the day, especially if their school does not include recess.

Lack of social/academic skills. If students do not have the social or academic skills that are required for a specific situation, misbehavior is likely. Just the anticipation of a frustrating task can trigger a 10-minute visit to the pencil sharpener. Cherise, who lives in a community where talking out indicates enthusiasm, is considered disruptive in her classroom where talking out without raising one's hand is not allowed. Carl, who does not have the math skills to compute the fraction problems, turns over the block bins rather than reveal to his teammates that he is unable to do the learning task. Jory, who lives in a house where parents and siblings lash out by yelling and punching at the slightest irritation, has never learned to use any other strategies when angry.

Tics and obsessive-compulsive behaviors. Motor and vocal tics are brief, sudden, purposeless, involuntary repetitive movements or sounds. Some common examples include eye blinking, shoulder shrugging, banging on a surface, mimicking of gestures, shouting, throat clearing, and barking noises. Tics often increase with stress and decrease with concentration on a task.

Obsessive-compulsive behaviors are involuntary recurrent behaviors or thoughts that the student feels must be done repeatedly. Examples include repeated hand washing, touching an object with one hand after touching it with the other, checking and rechecking things many times, and mentally counting over and over. Tics and obsessive-compulsive behaviors are no longer attributed to attitudes a person learned in childhood—for example, an inordinate emphasis on cleanliness or a dysfunctional family. Instead, the search for causes now focuses on the interaction of neurobiological factors, genetics, and environmental influences. Although students may suppress these behaviors for short time periods, eventually they have to let them out.

Substance abuse. Whenever a student is using alcohol, stimulants, inhalants, or other drugs, staff must consider whether misbehavior is directly linked to them. Stimulants and alcohol can trigger hostility and aggression, marijuana can trigger highly disruptive classroom clowning, and inhalants can trigger explosive rages. Because the list of substance abuse-disruptive behavior links is extensive, staff must always consider whether these connections are factors. Although students will often abuse drugs to satisfy another function on this list (as when Allison drinks alcohol because she seeks relief from guilt), we believe that the connection between misbehavior and substance abuse is so widespread in schools that the school team cannot afford to overlook it. The school staff will be able to develop a more effective intervention if they recognize the direct substance abuse as well as related functions.

Rhonda's Behavior Function Grid

The completed behavior function grid for Rhonda, a fifth grader (Exhibit 3.1), displays the relationship between her misbehaviors and the corresponding functions that her school team hypothesized were maintaining those behaviors. After observing the school environment, discussing the data, and talking with her parents, Rhonda's school team hypothesized the following:

1. Rhonda's aggression (pushing and tripping other students) during gym class appeared to be both a function of her wanting the gym teacher's attention and her overstimulation in the din of an enormous gym where four classes participated at the same time.

2. Both Rhonda's out-of-seat behavior (slowly ambling around the room until reminded to work at desk) and her inappropriate use of school materials (slamming books on desk, tearing papers into small pieces at her desk, playing football with her reading book) were a function of her wanting the teacher's attention and her lack of grade-level reading skills. Rhonda was far more likely to exhibit these behaviors whenever the class was asked to read a book or paper. If the teacher did not respond to her antics, Rhonda escalated her behavior and became more dramatic in her actions.

3. Rhonda's disorganized behaviors (not completing homework and not following along in the textbook with the rest of the class) appeared to occur because of her lack of grade-level reading skills.

Fortunately, Rhonda's school team took these behavior functions into account when they planned an intervention and enrolled her in an inclusion reading class that met daily before school. In this remedial reading course, both special education and regular education students with similar decoding problems received intensive daily instruction. After surveying the behavior function grid they had developed, the school team also made sure that extra time with a favorite teacher was included as one of the incentives in Rhonda's behavior program. Making a hypothesis about the functions of Rhonda's misbehavior enabled the school team to create an individualized behavior intervention that addressed some of the root causes of her misbehavior.

Once your team has completed these first six steps in the problem-solving process and has identified the probable function(s) of the student's misbehavior, you have officially completed a Functional Behavioral Assessment (FBA) and are ready to determine the specific interventions needed for resolution. The student's Functional Behavioral Assessment will serve as the bridge to the behavior intervention your team designs by helping you identify and plan for the environmental and instructional adaptations that will help him or her.

Step 7: Develop a Plan to Change the Unwanted Behavior

Almost any plan you develop will include behavioral as well as instructional, curricular, and environmental modifications to increase the likelihood of success. Although a researcher would want to proceed with only one change at a time in order to see if the unmanageable behavior was

EXHIBIT 3.1 Completed Behavior Function Grid

FUNCTION / BEHAVIOR	Leaving school grounds	Physical aggression	Disturbing others with hands, feet, objects	Disrespectful and/or threatening language	Inappropriate use of school materials	Talking out in class	Out of seat	Noncompliance	Inability to work independently	Disorganized behaviors			
Seek attention from peers and adults		X			X		X						
Seek tangible reinforcement													
Seek power over others													
Seek revenge													
Seek stimulation													
Avoid uncomfortable sensory stimulation		X											
Avoid fear													
Avoid guilt													
Need sleep, food, drink, or exercise													
Lack of social/academic skills					X		X			X			
Tics/Obsessive-compulsive behaviors													
Substance abuse													

Student: _Rhonda McMullin_   Date: _April 17, 1998_   Teacher: _Martha Salazar_

McEwan, E., & Damer, M. *Managing Unmanageable Students: Practical Solutions for Administrators.*
© 2000, Corwin Press, Inc.

then resolved, you are operating in a real-world environment. You need to resolve the problem as soon as possible, and your best chance for accomplishing that goal is trying out several well thought out changes as quickly as possible. Use the Action Plan Summary Form (Form 3.3) to describe your team's plan. Exhibit 3.2 is a sample action plan generated by one school team. Occasionally, a well-devised curricular, instructional, or environmental adaptation will solve a behavior problem without a specific behavior plan, as the following examples demonstrate.

Adaptations That Produce Results

Instructional and curricular adaptations. Although the teacher had labeled Seth "uncontrollable," the records showed that the majority of times that he was sent to the principal's office occurred either during math class or shortly after it ended. Observations by the principal and psychologist confirmed that although Seth was typically on-task more than 80% of the time during his other classes, during math he left his desk, made obnoxious noises, threw materials, poked other students, and did not complete work. When the school team scrutinized the math class they found that Seth predictably played with the manipulatives, especially if he was instructed to work with them while sitting with a group of four or five other students on the floor. He could not resist constructing a train with his blocks, pushing them around the floor whenever the teacher was helping another group. Because Seth was still unable to add or subtract quickly without counting on his fingers or using the blocks, solving some of the required problems took him much longer than the other children who knew their facts. The teacher's unstructured style added to his frustration level. Although classroom rules were posted, they were followed inconsistently and the teacher never referred to them.

Seth's teacher was convinced that Seth's behavior made him a suitable candidate for a behavior disorder classroom. Serious interventions were needed immediately. The team moved into action and proceeded through Steps 1 through 6 of the problem-solving process. As part of Step 7, they decided to recommend several significant instructional and curriculum adaptations that ranged from implementing an intensive math facts program for Seth and four of his classmates to providing a private desk carrel area in the corner of the classroom. The teacher planned to start each class period reminding students about the behavioral expectations for the class, and the assistant principal agreed to work with the teacher to ensure that she consistently followed classroom rules. In Seth's case, the team never had to pursue developing a formalized group behavior plan because he responded so well to the instructional and curricular changes.

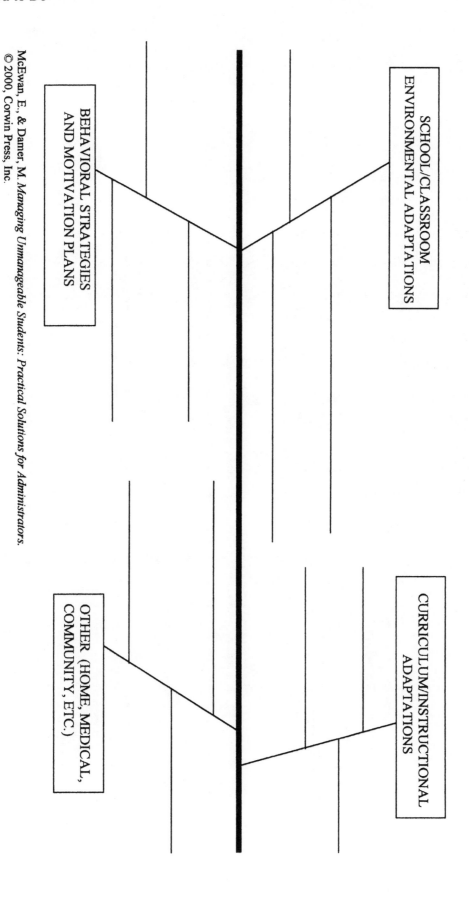

McEwan, E., & Damer, M. *Managing Unmanageable Students: Practical Solutions for Administrators.*
© 2000, Corwin Press, Inc.

FORM 3.3 Action Plan Summary Form

SCHOOL/CLASSROOM
ENVIRONMENTAL ADAPTATIONS

BEHAVIORAL STRATEGIES
AND MOTIVATION PLANS

OTHER (HOME, MEDICAL,
COMMUNITY, ETC.)

CURRICULUM/INSTRUCTIONAL
ADAPTATIONS

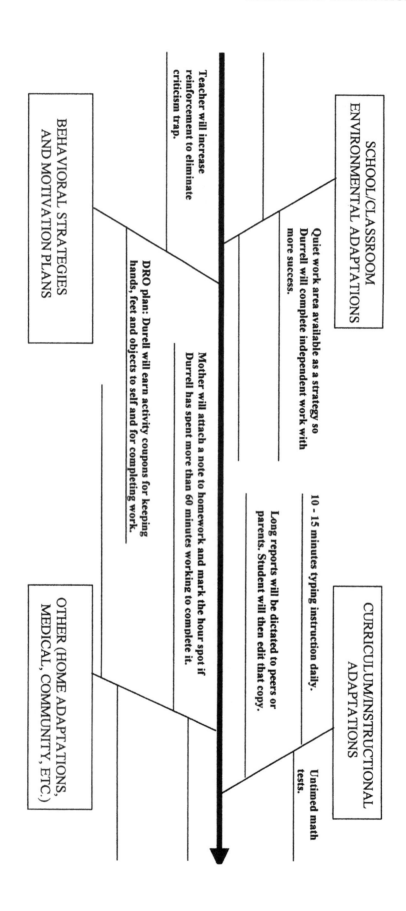

EXHIBIT 3.2   Completed Action Plan Summary Form

McEwan, E., & Damer, M. *Managing Unmanageable Students: Practical Solutions for Administrators.*
© 2000, Corwin Press, Inc.

SCHOOL/CLASSROOM
ENVIRONMENTAL ADAPTATIONS

Quiet work area available as a strategy so
Durrell will complete independent work with
more success.

Teacher will increase
reinforcement to eliminate
criticism trap.

BEHAVIORAL STRATEGIES
AND MOTIVATION PLANS

DRO plan: Durell will earn activity coupons for keeping
hands, feet and objects to self and for completing work.

Mother will attach a note to homework and mark the hour spot if
Durrell has spent more than 60 minutes working to complete it.

10 - 15 minutes typing instruction daily.

Long reports will be dictated to peers or
parents. Student will then edit that copy.

CURRICULUM/INSTRUCTIONAL
ADAPTATIONS

Untimed math
tests.

OTHER (HOME ADAPTATIONS,
MEDICAL, COMMUNITY, ETC.)

Environmental adaptations. Dorwin, an eighth-grade student, was repeatedly referred to the principal for fighting, pushing other students, and swearing at adults. When it became apparent that the collection of pink slips Dorwin had received could wallpaper his entire locker, the principal appointed a team to develop a plan. When the team gathered to analyze the problem, their observations and data showed that Dorwin's fighting and inability to keep hands and feet to himself almost always occurred prior to or during lunch period.

The school environment proved to be the trigger for Dorwin's behavior. A failed referendum had resulted in an overcrowded lunchroom that at times resembled a free-for-all as untrained lunch aides tried their best to keep order. The problems started right before lunch, when a massive group of eighth graders stood in a holding area outside the cafeteria waiting for the signal to enter. Dorwin had a hair-trigger automatic fight response whenever another student jostled an elbow into his arm or pushed against his back.

Although the cafeteria situation seemed unlikely to improve given the district's financial situation, as staff brainstormed during Step 7 they arrived at a number of solutions to reduce the chaos during lunchtime—solutions that the principal would need to coordinate. The 5-minute "holding area" had to be discontinued, requiring teachers to dismiss their students for lunch a few minutes later. Cafeteria aides whose only communication with students was yelling at them needed training to learn how to be assertive with students without producing unproductive confrontations. Rules and consequences for the lunchroom had to be established, posted, and consistently followed. Choosing to sit with one's friends needed to be considered a privilege and not an assumed right. Until changes were made to the cafeteria environment, developing a behavior intervention specifically for Dorwin seemed a waste of time. Actually, once the school cafeteria became more orderly, predictable, and quieter, Dorwin no longer was aggressive to other students or rude to staff. The environmental adaptations that coincidentally benefited all students were also the perfect solution to Dorwin's problem.

Behavioral Interventions

In most cases, curricular, instructional, or environmental interventions are not sufficient to change a student's behavior. A well-designed behavior management plan must also be developed. The following are five different types of behavior management plans to consider: (a) Rewarding/Motivating Desirable Behaviors, (b) Rewarding/Motivating Absence of Disruptive Behaviors, (c) Punishing Disruptive Behaviors, (d) Teaching Desirable Behaviors, and (e) Ignoring Disruptive Behaviors.

Although these plans may sound complicated and somewhat ominous, you no doubt already employ many of the interventions in your school. When you honor a Student-of-the-Week, you are motivating or rewarding desirable behavior. When teachers give As or Bs for good work, they are giving a different type of reward. Losing recess, staying after school, or contacting parents are punishments that all teachers employ. Ms. Billing's use of assertive discipline with its warning checks on the blackboard is another type of punishment. Just this afternoon you ignored the first grade's loud talking in the hall, even though a school rule states no talking in the halls. You knew the students were excited about the afternoon pet show assembly and drawing attention to the behavior might only serve to exacerbate the problem.

For most of the students in your school, these routine interventions—rewarding, giving consequences, or ignoring—are effective in preventing disruptive behavior, especially if staff members are consistent and fair in the ways they use them. But, these methods that are effective with the majority of your students do not seem to make an impact on students with unmanageable behaviors. Whether the motivation is not strong enough, the punishment too haphazard, or the ignoring inconsistent is hard to determine. What is clear, however, is that more and better interventions are needed. The behavior interventions that your staff plans for the unmanageable student will require more consistency and strategic planning if they are to succeed. Chapters 4 and 5 offer many practical suggestions for developing and implementing the first three types of plans. Behavior plans that employ teaching and ignoring are less common and are mentioned here briefly.

Your team will occasionally select a teaching intervention, especially if a social worker or speech pathologist participates in the team meeting. If the team determines that the function of Marissa's behavior is to protest, but that she does not know how to be assertive without being aggressive, the team could decide that assertiveness training might be an effective intervention. If Marissa's parents agree, the social worker might meet twice a week with Marissa to teach her how to disagree with another student through role playing activities. The goal is to enable Marissa to solve problems without resorting to her current "Jerry Springer" style of yelling and intimidation.

If Jason's shoving and pushing appear to be related to his inability to play with his first-grade classmates, the speech pathologist, whom he is currently seeing for articulation practice, might volunteer to begin teaching him how to ask other children to share the swings or play a game of ball.

Occasionally, if the team believes that a student is being disruptive to gain attention, they will opt to intervene by systematically ignoring his or her unmanageable behavior. Because ignoring has as great a chance of increasing or intensifying a behavior as decreasing it, this option must be used with caution. The teacher has to brace for a short upsurge since a disruptive behavior will always increase immediately after everyone starts to ignore it. Ignoring should only be used for behaviors that can be tolerated during the upsurge period and is usually selected for teacher-irritant behaviors rather than high-priority behaviors such as aggression, which cannot be tolerated.

If staff members observed that whenever Ricardo screamed in his kindergarten class, the teacher's assistant held and rocked him soothingly, they might decide to see if he is throwing tantrums to get this type of attention. The intervention they plan will require that the assistant and the teacher ignore the tantrums. Because ignoring always works best with a motivation intervention, the team should plan to have the classroom assistant give extra time and attention to Ricardo when he is contentedly working on a school project and not screaming. If ignoring is to be a successful intervention, the teacher will have to endure a few days of increased tantrums before they become a rare occurrence. If the intervention is unsuccessful, the initial surge will continue to increase in frequency and intensity. Anytime that an ignoring intervention is chosen, the team must be prepared to switch gears if classroom disruption is unacceptable.

One of the authors once worked with a school team whose ignoring intervention required the entire first grade class to leave and go outside for a walk if Tyrel had another tantrum. Although this idea seemed ludicrous to the teacher when she first heard of it, because the principal volunteered to watch Tyrel in the classroom until the tantrum stopped, she agreed to use the ignoring intervention for a week or two. Several days later, when the principal was observing in the classroom as Tyrel had his longest and loudest tantrum ever, she wondered about the wisdom of this intervention to which she had agreed. Fortunately, Tyrel's second tantrum on the next day did not last long and it turned out to be his last tantrum of the school year. When Tyrel stopped receiving undo attention from the children and his teachers for his earsplitting screaming, his tantrums stopped serving their function. Although an ignoring intervention can have this positive effect, the only way this school team could ever know for sure that it would resolve the problem was to try it.

Ignoring is almost always a preferred choice for neurologically based behaviors, which will only increase if attention is paid to them. The student who has a vocal tic (e.g., standing up at his desk and shouting out a word or two), or a student with obsessive-compulsive behavior (e.g., flicking the lights on and off when entering or leaving a room) is best ignored. If the teacher tries to stop the tic or the obsessive-compulsive behavior, it is likely either to increase or be held back until the child bursts out with even more explosive behavior. Although ignoring these behaviors will take some effort from the teacher and students during the first few days, soon they will tune them out.

The Fairness Issue

If teachers on your staff have never developed a formal plan to resolve a student's unmanageable behavior, their first reaction is fear that making such adaptations for one student is not fair to all the others. They are convinced that other students will be angry that the child who has been disrupting their class has been singled out for special attention. Teachers sometimes worry that the other students will begin to adopt some of the difficult behaviors. As you listen to their protests, you find yourself wondering if they are projecting their own feelings onto what they claim the other students will feel. Be assured that after one or two teachers on your staff have resolved a particularly difficult student's unmanageable behaviors, the fairness issue will become moot. Until that time, you can help your teaching staff with this issue by making the following points.

1. *Assure them that a behavior intervention and accompanying adaptations are only successful if, in the long run, they save time for the teacher.* Help them reflect on how much time and energy they are currently spending on students with unmanageable behaviors. Even though the initial process is time consuming, the whole purpose of an intervention plan is to eliminate the problems and allow the teacher to gain that time and energy. In the long run, all students will benefit if behavior problems are resolved.

2. *Remind the teachers that other students feel threatened when they perceive that the teacher does not have control of a student who is disruptive.* Even if the disruptive behaviors are not directed at them, students feel threatened in a chaotic environment where their teacher is ineffective with one of the students in class. Reassure your teachers that rather than resenting the extra attention paid to the difficult student, the other students in their classrooms will become their most ardent cheerleaders if they manage to resolve the behavior problems.

3. *Warn the teachers that a few students may whine about the fairness issue on the first day or two the plan is implemented and that the teachers' initial response to the whining will determine whether those students cease their manipulation.* Encourage teachers to talk with students about the concepts of individual strengths and weaknesses. Suggest that teachers ask for a few students to give examples of their own strengths and weaknesses. Once this conversation has been introduced, teachers can explain that when individuals have difficulty doing something, they often need extra help in the beginning until they learn to do it. The teacher can give examples of a child who needed extra math tutoring to learn the multiplication tables or a batter who needed to stand closer to the pitcher in gym class. The teacher can matter-of-factly explain that because following the school or classroom rules has been difficult for Joanne, the teacher wants to try something different on Monday that may be more helpful for her. At that point, the teacher can provide some details about the new plan.

Your team's intervention plan will have a better chance of success if the team prepares in advance for any difficulties that might arise. If the team has selected an ignoring intervention, everyone should discuss what the teacher should do if the disruptive behavior increases. If the team has selected a teaching intervention, discussion should focus on how the teacher can help Marissa use her newly learned assertiveness skills in real-life situations. What can the teacher say when she begins swearing at another student to express her disagreement? Unless the teacher reminds Marissa to use the "calm down" strategy she has learned from the social worker, she will probably not practice the recently introduced assertiveness skills.

To prevent misunderstanding and procrastination, make a list of who does what and by when before the end of the team meeting. If you have delegated the responsibility of gatekeeper or recorder, that person can also assume the responsibility for this necessary team function. If you determine clearly when the plan will go into effect and who needs to make what specific changes or complete certain activities by that time, you will prevent glitches in planning that can sabotage the best designed plan. The recorder should distribute a copy of the final list of responsibilities to the staff within a day or two following the meeting so that everyone knows his or her part of the plan. This list will guide the team to Steps 8 and 9, setting a specific date and procedure for evaluating the plan. One team listed the following responsibilities before they left their planning meeting:

1. The team plan for Bobby will begin on February 20, 1 week from the team meeting.

2. Ms. Hauser, the main classroom teacher, will design daily point sheets and keep track of the percentage points earned weekly, especially noting the times when Bobby was not successful.

3. Ms. Hauser will develop a written room chart listing the three new rules.

4. Ms. Hauser will design the reinforcement menu and give a copy to Bobby.

5. Mr. Fatheree, the school principal, will provide funds and direct the media specialist to purchase additional computer games for the classroom.

6. Mr. Fatheree will arrange for Bobby's inclusion in the math class one grade level below his current one that is still working on subtraction with borrowing.

7. Ms. Samuels, the school psychologist, will explain the changes to Bobby before February 20th and discuss details of the motivational plan with his parents within the next 2 days.

8. Ms. Samuels will also talk to Bobby's mother about whether the school can communicate directly with the doctor who prescribes his medication to provide documentation and an update on some of the behaviors that are occurring at school.

9. Mr. Fatheree and Ms. Samuels will observe the plan in action during the week of February 20th and provide feedback to teachers on their observations.

10. Unless the team determines that a follow-up meeting should be scheduled earlier, the team will meet to evaluate the plan's effectiveness on March 22 immediately after the school day ends.

11. Ms. Hauser will provide the team with a summary sheet at that time, detailing Bobby's points earned during the month. Mr. Fatheree and Ms. Samuels will both observe Bobby at least twice during the final week before the follow-up meeting and bring in their observations.

Step 8: Implement the Plan

Once the starting date for the intervention plan arrives, your duties will be similar to those of the teacher in your school who coordinates the spring play. You are the director. If one staff member does not fulfill an assigned responsibility, the entire show could close early. It is your job to make sure everyone learns and performs his or her part.

The Stage Is Set

Assigning responsibilities is the first aspect of actual implementation. In the case of the team's plan for Bobby, there were a number of tasks assigned: (a) placement of Bobby in a new math class, (b) developing a point sheet, and (c) purchasing and installing new computer games in the classroom. Each task must be completed in a timely fashion.

The Actors/Actresses Have Learned Their Parts

If the team recommended that Bobby's teacher reposition his desk to the front of the room and use more focusing cues to direct his attention to seatwork, the teacher has to turn over a new leaf and integrate a different set of teaching behaviors into her repertoire. When old habits need changing, your staff is faced with the most difficult aspect of implementing a plan. Often, the teacher will be unable to change ingrained behaviors and habits without your monitoring, feedback, and support.

The Director Has the Script in Hand

Effective monitoring can be as simple as visiting the classroom once every few days to sit and observe for a few minutes. Later, when you converse with the teacher you can mention the positive aspects of the intervention that you saw in the classroom. To ensure that staff is following through, drop in to the classroom or psychologist's office before or after school and ask to see the reinforcement menu or inquire how the conversation with mom and dad went. Your interest in all of the details of the plan's implementation will in itself raise the accountability level of team members.

If your interest and casual attention do not ensure that staff members meet intervention plan responsibilities, then you will need to use more assertive and/or creative monitoring techniques. If the day before the intervention plan begins you find out that the psychologist did not meet the deadline to call the parents, firmly request that he or she put other tasks aside until the parent has been contacted. If you observe that the teacher has not stopped the barrage of criticism habitually given to the target student, let him know that you will help by visiting the classroom periodically to observe how many times he criticizes versus how often he says anything complimentary. If the teacher is still unable to change those critical patterns, you may decide to have someone videotape one of his classes so that later you can sit down and count the criticisms together. Your role as an instructional leader is vital in helping staff members change teaching behaviors that they are unable to change on their own.

Step 9: Figure Out If the Plan Has Worked and Change It If Necessary

Step 10: Decide What to Do Next

If your team set a date for the follow-up meeting at the outset and also predetermined who would observe and record data during the implementation, you are ready for the evaluation meeting. Begin the meeting by comparing the most recent data to that collected before the plan was used. Has Troy's on-task behavior in the classroom increased and by how much? Has he received fewer pink slips in the school cafeteria? Is he now more compliant in following the teacher's instructions? How often does he earn the expected number of points?

In preparation for the follow-up meeting, Troy's teacher prepared a graph showing the percentage of points Troy earned each day of implementation. A student who does not experience a certain measure of success with the plan will either just shrug his shoulders and ignore it or act out with greater frequency as a result of the frustration. The teacher noted that Troy had been earning only 40% of the points that were possible. The team discussed whether to follow the psychologist's suggestion that Troy be able to exchange his points at the end of the week for a choice of rewards. One teacher disagreed, arguing that Troy would need to exchange the points every day. She did not think that Troy had the self-control to wait an entire week for his reward. Noting Troy's lack of success, the team decided to switch to a daily exchange of points for rewards for 2 weeks to see if he responded to a more immediate and concrete reward structure.

We cannot give you a formula for determining whether a plan has resolved your unmanageable student's behavior problem. Having a model student emerge one month after beginning a plan happens only once every 10 to 20 years, but the data from classroom observation should show a change in a positive direction. If the student is earning points as motivation for improved behavior, the team members need to know the percentage of daily points he has earned in comparison to the total he might have earned if his behavior met the standard set up in advance by the team. If a student earns below an average of 80% of the possible daily points, the behavior intervention will predictably not resolve the unmanageable behavior. When the student is not earning an average of 80% of the possible number of daily points, team members have to determine whether they designed an intervention that was too challenging from the start or whether the student is just not responding to the motivation plan.

As team members determine whether their plan has been successful, they will also need to consider the priority level of a student's behavior. Because high-priority behavior poses a threat to the student or to other students, in order to be considered successful a plan must produce more dramatic results. Only low levels or no levels of the behavior can be tolerated. A successful plan to resolve behavior problems for a student who punches out other students or who runs away from the school building has to bring about rapid change. A successful plan to resolve a student's out-of-seat behavior can tolerably bring about more gradual change, depending on how disruptive the student is to the rest of the classroom.

If a team's plan has been successful, the environmental, instructional, and curricular adaptations will probably remain in place for the rest of the year if not for several years to come. Perhaps your team suggested that a first grader who was disrupting math classes every day be moved into a third grade math classroom resulting in a cessation of the disruptive behavior. Because it appears that the student's disruptive behavior was a response to boredom, you need to ensure that next year he is put into a more challenging math class from the very first day of school. A student who has responded well to having a separate, nondistracting work area will benefit from this type of adaptation for the rest of his school career.

In contrast, if team members planned a more formal behavior intervention that has helped to resolve a problem, they will want to begin planning how to gradually wean the student away from the plan over a period of time. Unless they build in this weaning process, the student is likely to relapse and resume the undesirable behaviors if the next teacher does not use the intervention. If an intervention in which Katina earns points so that she can help out in the kindergarten room has been successful, at the first follow-up meeting the team will probably want to continue the point rewards to ensure that her success continues. At a third follow-up meeting, 2 or 3 months later, the team may decide to make the intervention more challenging. Rather than earning points for every half-hour without noncompliance, now Katina will start earning them hourly. She will need to earn three more points to earn the privilege to go to the kindergarten. Katina's team believes that she is ready for more challenge and will still be able to earn at least 80% of the points if they make those changes. Eventually, Katina's team would like to see her earning points at weekly intervals before moving on to a self-reporting system. She has done so well up until now that everyone believes that within 7 months she might no longer even need the formal point system. Her team will continue to recommend, however, that her teachers permit her to type all of her papers rather than write them with her illegible, labored script.

Routine follow-up meetings should take no longer than 20 minutes and can be held during a regularly scheduled block of time. Unless the parents have been invited, the team member who has most closely worked with them should apprise them of the school's efforts, updating the student's progress or lack of it.

What to Do If Nothing Is Working

There will always be a very small percentage of students for whom nothing seems to work. The best laid plans and the most consistent follow-through activities produce nothing but frustration for everyone concerned. These are signals that other options must be explored. Following are some alternatives to consider:

1. Hire a behavior management consultant to observe the student and work with your school team to develop a brand-new plan.
2. Discuss placing the student in a different or more structured environment for a portion or all of the school day.
3. Refer the student to a pediatric neurologist.
4. Consider placement in a public school alternative school.
5. Consider a private placement.

Developing interventions and implementing them is demanding and time consuming. If you hire a behavior management consultant to handle your most challenging cases, you will prevent burnout, discouragement, and cynicism on the part of your staff. Everyone needs to feel successful, and when the team is failing the time has come to call in reinforcements.

Perhaps the student in question might benefit from a change in placement that could involve an assignment to another classroom teacher who will be able to provide the type of structure and expectations that are essential to success. A decision of this nature is likely to raise the hackles of some staff members who always interpret a decision to change a child's regular classroom teacher as giving in to parents' pressure or giving a child what he wants. We have not found this to be the case. There are some student-teacher combinations that are explosive and a change in assignment is the only answer. Another type of placement change might include a temporary or permanent assignment to a self-contained classroom.

In some cases, an unmanageable student is suffering from a physiological, emotional, or psychological disorder that must be addressed by medication or more sophisticated treatments. If your resource file includes the name of at least one skilled pediatric neurologist who stays on top of the rapid advances in that field, this individual should be your first choice. If this is not an option, then consider a child psychiatrist, a behavioral psychologist, or a team of doctors (usually at a hospital or clinic) who pool their expertise to consider particularly challenging cases.

Drew's story demonstrates how a school district staff resolved a seemingly unsolvable behavior problem through medical intervention. Drew was the most difficult student the principal had ever encountered. He was rarely on-task for more than 3 or 4 minutes, refused to do anything the teacher asked him to do, made siren noises in class, and threw stones at the other students during recess. He held students on the playground spellbound when he advised them not to listen to the teacher because she was a "big brat" and that he was going to kill her. None of the strategies that school personnel tried with Drew made a dent in these aberrant behaviors. Hiring a special aide to accompany Drew throughout his day only ensured that other students did not get hurt, but did nothing to help Drew.

The teacher's reward program increased the number of malicious comments he screamed at her, and the principal's idea to send Drew home whenever he hit or pushed caused that behavior to skyrocket. Even the behavior consultant's intensive 5-minute interval reward program seemed to have no effect. When the staff considered the only alternative school for extremely disruptive children, they thought of the hour-long bus ride and wondered how soon Drew would either cause the driver to quit or have an accident. This angry second grader was siphoning off everyone's energy and time.

Only later did the staff have the hindsight to wish that they had heeded the nurse's advice to "get thee to a good neurologist" sooner. Fortunately, the principal had developed a good relationship with Drew's parents during the many times they met to talk about the latest plan or share stories of frustration. When the staff proposed consulting with a neurologist, the parents were willing to follow the recommendation. The school nurse called immediately and convinced the neurologist to squeeze in an emergency case, thereby bypassing the usual 2-month wait. The social worker found a source of funding for this low-income family, and the principal faxed the data on the frequency and type of behavior seen at school to the neurologist. Parents and school worked closely in what had become an emergency situation. Two weeks later the neurologist's diagnosis of Manic Depressive Disorder came as a surprise to everyone, although the parents realized later that the older brother who was now in jail probably had the same condition. The diagnosis also revealed that the Ritalin™ prescribed for Drew by the local family doctor had exacerbated his condition, triggering some of his extreme aggression.

A month later, when the new medication was working at full strength, Drew seemed to be a different child at school. Although he still had challenging behaviors, now he had the self-control to respond to the reward program and learn alternative ways to react to frustration. The school team developed a plan to phase out the one-on-one aide and Drew's academic achievement soared. Finally, the principal could turn all of her time and energy to other projects that had been languishing.

Inherent in recommending that parents seek medical advice is the legal responsibility for bearing the cost. We have found that in such circumstances, resources to cover the cost of a neurological work-up can usually be secured by a creative social worker or counselor (e.g., social services, scholarship funds, or an educational foundation). This is an option that should not be recommended lightly, but must be considered in the case of a highly challenging student.

When every other option has been exhausted, a private placement in an alternative school or a special facility must be considered.

It Is Not as Hard as You Might Think

Before you can fine-tune your plan, you will benefit from carefully reading Chapters 4 and 5. They discuss the controversy surrounding behavior management, detail the specific advantages and pitfalls of rewards and punishments, and offer practical examples that your team can adapt.

Chapter 4 contains essential information about rewards and how to use them effectively in developing behavioral intervention plans. You will be introduced to Greg, a typical student with unmanageable behaviors, and find out how his school's team developed a DRO (Differential Reinforcement of Omission of Behavior) plan. This plan is a combination of two of the types of behavioral plans mentioned earlier: Rewarding/Motivating Desirable Behaviors and Rewarding/Motivating Absence of Disruptive Behaviors. A sample of the plan is included in Chapter 4.

Chapter 5 describes what punishment is and how you can make it work for you. You will meet John and learn how his teachers put together a response cost plan that combined mild punishment of his disruptive behaviors with rewards.

If you are a bit overwhelmed as you consider the enormity of the problems and the complexity of the solutions, you are a realist. We do not promise instant results or magical behavioral transformations without hard work and consistency. We hope you also feel energized at the prospects for improvement in the climate and morale of your school that a few successful interventions could bring. The benefits will spill over into other areas of school life as well. When instruction improves for an unmanageable student, it improves for every student in a teacher's classroom. When a group of staff members learns to plan collaboratively regarding an unmanageable student, these same skills will bring benefits at grade-level team meetings or in goal-setting for the coming year. Once you have begun to use this problem-solving process, you may want to offer additional staff development in team building and shared decision making.

There will be staff members who are resistant, and you may need some subtle or even more overt behavior intervention plans for unmanageable teachers. There will be students who are especially difficult; you may need to consult with behavioral or medical specialists for assistance. This process does not have a beginning and an end. It is messy and often as unmanageable as the students for whom it was designed, but with leadership and persistence, you will succeed.

CHAPTER FOUR

Rewards and How to Use Them Effectively

Even though the economic, legal, and moral foundations of the Western world are based on the notion that people ought to be rewarded for hard work and good deeds and ought to be punished for laziness and evil, these concepts have fallen on hard times. The natural empathy of practitioners combined with the beliefs of many socially concerned theorists have created an environment in which educators are reluctant to hold students accountable for what they do and accordingly, reluctant to offer rewards for personal accomplishments. But, you cannot manage the behavior of unmanageable students without understanding how rewards and punishments work and how to use them effectively.

Rewards and How They Work

Alfie Kohn, author of the popular book, *Punished by Rewards: The Trouble With Stars, Incentive Plans, A's, Praise, and Other Bribes* (1993), believes that "all rewards, by virtue of being rewards, are not attempts to influence or persuade or solve problems together, but simply to control" (p. 27). Many educators have eagerly embraced Kohn's views, attempting to eliminate rewards from their schools and classrooms. These "Kohnites" are afraid to praise students for their actions because by using such undue control they may inhibit the students' interest in learning. You or some of your staff members may believe that the use of any rewards is manipulative and underhanded.

We, on the other hand, unequivocally agree with Ken Blanchard who insists

> if there's one thing I've learned in my life it's the fact that everyone
> wants to be appreciated. This goes for managers as well as employ-

ees, parents as well as children, and coaches as well as players. We never outgrow this need and even if it looks like we are independent and self-sufficient, the fact is we need others to help us feel valued. (Nelson, 1994, p. ix)

The rewards for unmanageable students come in the form of what is called positive reinforcement. These are consequences presented by the teacher or school that maintain or strengthen a student's behavior over time. Reinforcing consequences can include praise, a no-homework day, or coupons that are given to encourage students to complete independent work, walk quietly in the halls, or answer questions in class. It will not be easy to convince teachers that rewards have merits if they admire Kohn's work and if their basic assumptions are grounded in psychological theories that discourage positive reinforcement for work well done. You are up against a theory that assumes any earned self-esteem a child develops as a result of reinforcement is harmful. In helping school staff work with unmanageable children, we have encountered this seemingly insurmountable resistance so frequently that we suggest four effective ways to move past it.

Ways to Overcome Resistance to the Use of Positive Reinforcement

Model Positive Reinforcement as You Lead

First, make sure that you model effective reinforcement through your own actions. When we are working with teachers who are initially opposed to reinforcing students for their on-task behaviors and efforts, we ask them to brainstorm four or five inexpensive things that their building principals could do to motivate them to work harder. Suddenly they are more receptive to the benefits of praise and rewards! Teachers often describe their anger and frustration at working in school environments in which their efforts and accomplishments are rarely acknowledged. They describe a visceral aching for reinforcement. Even the most conscientious teachers admit that they would give even more effort for a principal who acknowledges their best efforts and successes. Over the years we have asked teachers how their principal could reward their efforts to work successfully with an unmanageable child or to develop more sophisticated lesson plans. The following suggestions should provide a guide for helping you increase your own use of reinforcement with staff:

1. Flowers

2. Closest parking space to the door for a month

3. Secretarial time

4. Extra photocopying funds

5. Post-it® note with praise for successful efforts

6. Special lunch

7. Being asked to present latest project at monthly meeting

8. Letter of praise in file and to the superintendent

9. Article in newspaper about latest effort

10. Principal substitute-teaches for an hour in classroom

Keep these suggestions in mind when you want to affirm and appreciate your staff members.

In addition to positively affirming the contributions of your staff as a whole, you may also have to model more assertive positive reinforcement as you respond to a difficult teacher. Your staff will be watching you closely as you modify your personal feelings of anger or stress in response to the behavior of an ineffective, difficult teacher. Whenever you hear Lydia Samuels harangue a disruptive student in her class for not completing the homework that is too difficult for his skill level, resist the impulse to grind your teeth and grimace. Ignore your instinctive reactions either to criticize or completely ignore Lydia. To change Lydia Samuels' punitive habits of a lifetime, determine what motivates her and acknowledge her sputtering attempts to change those habits. Part of your plan should include a frank discussion with the teacher, but unless you also use reinforcement, the most powerful tool at your disposal, neither staff development nor threats of remediation will be successful. Without sincere, timely praise, Ms. Samuels may tenaciously resist all efforts to change her behavior.

Change the Name

If your staff is resistant to the concept of positive reinforcement, its association with behavioral psychology may be part of the problem. Many teachers who are opposed to positive reinforcement are unaware that they frequently use this tool, albeit haphazardly. Unfortunately, those teachers rarely use positive reinforcement with their most challenging students whom it would benefit most. We have found that teachers who resist the idea of reinforcing students will be more receptive if you recommend that they do any of the following:

- Appreciate students' accomplishments and efforts
- Provide positive, logical, or natural consequences to students
- Honor students' accomplishments and efforts
- Provide positive feedback to students

- Provide students with rewards for challenges they meet
- Praise students' accomplishments
- Affirm students' efforts
- Provide positive strokes

Positive reinforcement should be given as a result of a student's appropriate school behavior that your staff members want to encourage, and the end result should be that the student does more of that appropriate school behavior. You can pragmatically call the resulting reinforcement consequence by any name that is more palatable to your teachers.

Train and Teach Your Staff

Educate your staff about positive reinforcement so they can eventually understand how earned self-esteem develops when students' success in their struggle to learn new material or to work on more acceptable school behaviors is celebrated and acknowledged. Plan workshops, form study groups, and show videotapes that demonstrate the effectiveness of positive reinforcement. You will find some of the most convincing practical applications of reinforcement in the business world.

Demonstrate the Results

Some teachers are reluctant to use behavior management plans because of the increased work. Others perceive the use of a plan for one student as being unfair to the rest of the class. Explain that planned reinforcement can help challenging students learn productive behavior and work habits as well as develop positive feelings about school and self. Help reluctant teachers to move past their doubts by inviting them to talk with a "miracle worker" staff member. Choose an individual who can relate a shining success story to reassure the doubters that if they matter-of-factly explain the need for a positive reinforcement plan to their students when they introduce it, the others in class will quickly come to accept it.

Show teachers how the use of increased positive reinforcement during the times of day that are most problematic (e.g., transitions, journal writing, or the introduction of a new concept) can make their lives less stressful and their teaching more effective.

Our Favorite Reinforcement Ideas

Schools routinely give away or throw away some of the privileges and activities that students find most motivating. The key to selecting effective positive reinforcers is in knowing what motivates the individual student.

The school team working with Todd, who broke school materials and pushed peers, eliminated those behaviors by giving him the opportunity to feed the pet hamster down the hall. Michael's aggressive playground behavior was reduced dramatically by letting him earn the chance to clean the classroom sinks, tables, and shelves. Nothing else the staff tried had been as motivating as tackling those windows with glass cleaner. Emily's off-task chatting during social studies was no longer a problem once the teacher began to reward students who followed classroom rules with the opportunity to play drill games at the blackboard during the last 5 minutes of class.

Often, a parent provides the best information about potential motivators. Other clues can be picked up from the student's age and peer interests. Verbal praise to younger children should be expressed with an awe-filled change of expression. In contrast, middle school and high school students often prefer private praise that is given out of earshot of peers. The adult's tone should be adjusted to the older student's sense of coolness, avoiding undo inflection. Some masterful high school and middle school teachers deliver reinforcing puns and related jokes in response to student behaviors that they want to praise. These Robin Williams-clones are born not made, and their puns and jokes become the reinforcement for which students work. In these classrooms, the observer will notice students working their hardest for the teacher's stamp of approval, which routinely sets the class to laughing.

Some positive reinforcers can easily be interspersed naturally throughout the day. Others require special planning and coordination. Following are some of our favorites:

1. *Earning the right to play on the percussion instruments in the band room for 15 minutes or earning an extra gym class.* These motivating options that involve coordinating staff require a creative and supportive principal.

2. *Earning the opportunity to pick a Nintendo or Play Station "Game Tip" out of a designated Tip Box.* Teachers can cut out game tips that are routinely included in gaming magazines and put them into a decorated box.

3. *Earning the opportunity to help the school custodian or school secretary.* Many of the students sent to the office develop an affectionate relationship with the school secretary and unconsciously seek out ways to visit him or her in the midst of the exciting hubbub of activity—your office. The punishment of being sent to the office becomes negative reinforcement for these students, and they want to go as often as they can. Avoid inadvertently encouraging more disruptive behavior by using a punishment that is actually reinforcement. Turn these situations around and create opportunities to earn the right to spend time in the office helping the secretary.

4. *Earning extra responsibility.* Some younger students will work their hardest to be line leader, feed the class pet or water the flowers, be the teacher's official pencil sharpener, and deliver messages to the office. Older students will often work just as hard to volunteer in a younger classroom, help the custodian wipe tables after lunch, or assist a teacher in constructing a bulletin board. One student who was on the verge of going to a behavior disorders program in seventh grade turned around her attitude once the teacher told her she could earn a daily pass to help out in the special education classroom for profoundly handicapped students. This opportunity propelled the student to do her best.

5. *Earning the opportunity to have a no-homework day on Fridays.* An unexpected vacation from responsibilities is always welcome.

6. *Writing on the blackboard, drawing on the blackboard with colored chalk, solving a problem at the blackboard, working the overhead projector, making a transparency for the overhead projector, or photocopying the teacher's handouts for the next day.* Adults forget how much fun some of our most tedious activities are for students, even those in middle and high schools.

7. *Earning 2 minutes of chat time at the end of class.* Students never have enough time to socialize with friends. This is a favorite.

8. *Seeing progress depicted on a visual display.* Adults who have been motivated to lose weight or stop smoking by keeping daily charts and watching their progress can understand how reinforcing it is to watch one's progress. Older students often enjoy filling in a graph depicting the points they have earned or the increasing number of classes in which they have followed the rules. Younger students like to see depictions of their progress that are less abstract. A younger student might earn a length of construction paper to put up on the wall with the goal of eventually "tying up the room." Another favorite graphic display for a younger child might involve earning points to move the Lion King toward his lair on a colorful bulletin board display.

9. *Earning a special privilege for the classroom.* In addition to frustrating teachers, some of our most challenging students have had no social success with their peers. For some of these students, having the opportunity to earn a pizza party or a new computer game for the classroom becomes motivating.

10. *Earning time to play video games or computer games.* Fifteen years ago, middle school boys were the single most difficult group of students to motivate. One of the authors attended an entire seminar devoted to this problem, because at the time behavior consultants received the majority of their referrals for that population. During the presentation, a behavior consultant told of desperately devising a point system so that students

could earn plastic vomit, a plan that was wildly successful. Fortunately, the last decade has brought about an abundance of motivating video and computer games that once screened by your staff for language and violence, can provide the linchpin for any motivational program. An accommodating learning center coordinator can help the classroom teacher arrange times and security for the video reinforcers.

If a student is earning points that he or she will later trade for reinforcers, teachers can increase flexibility by developing a packet of coupons like the example in Exhibit 4.1. Coupons are a timely reinforcer that the student will actually receive later. If the student chooses to earn 20 minutes of playing a computer game in the learning center, the teacher can give the coupon at 11:00 in the morning even though the student will not have the necessary free time until 2:30 in the afternoon. The student can also take a coupon home if his or her parent has agreed that television or computer privileges will be earned only if behavior in school warrants it.

Positive Reinforcement Guidelines

When you suggest using positive reinforcement, a teacher might object, "But I used reinforcement with Timothy and it didn't work. I even tried using points so he could go on the class field trip." If so, your first task will be to investigate how effectively the teacher used the reinforcement. Positive reinforcement is a powerful tool, but only if basic guidelines are followed.

Always Provide Specific Verbal Feedback

The person who is giving the positive reinforcement (articulating the praise, giving the activity reward, assigning a point) should always tell the student specifically why it has been earned; for example, "I noticed how you worked on your assignment for the entire 15 minutes" or "You've earned all of your organization points for this class—all of your materials were here and you were on time for class," or "You worked so hard in the literature circle today and contributed some interesting ideas."

Teachers' praise should describe the specific behavior that they want to encourage. The praise should sound sincere and be accompanied by a change of expression or voice inflection. Robotic praise given by a teacher in the same tone of voice as directions to walk down the hall is not likely to be interpreted by the student as praise. Sometimes when teachers use point systems, they forget or think that it is unimportant to tell the student specifically why he or she earned each point. They will put the point on a chart without praising the student for earning it. Sometimes they feel awkward identifying a positive behavior that they take for granted with other students. In your monitoring role, remind teachers that their verbal feedback identifying the specific positive behavior, is as important as the point earned.

This coupon is good for:

_____ Student can delete 4 problems from math homework and still get full credit.

This coupon is good for:

_____ Student can choose one of Ms. Papke's "Had A Great Day" notes to bring home to parents.

This coupon is good for:

_____Student has earned 5 minutes of listening to Walkman.

This coupon is good for:

_____Student has earned 10 minutes of free time on computer in learning center.

This coupon is good for:

_____ 1/5 credit toward One-Break Card. When you have collected five of these coupons, you will earn a One-Break Card that will excuse you one time if you have a late assignment or forget to bring your materials to class.

This coupon is good for:

_____ 1/4 credit toward a fast-food free burger coupon. When you have collected four of these coupons, you will earn your ticket toward "fast food" heaven.

This coupon is good for:

_____ 1/2 credit toward a pencil. When you have collected two of these coupons, you can select a pencil from the supply shelf.

This coupon is good for:

_____Student can select the review game that the entire class will play on either Wednesdays or Fridays.

This coupon is good for:

_____ 1/5 credit toward video-taping the class in action on Friday. When you have collected five of these coupons, you can run the video camera, taping the Friday class.

This coupon is good for:

_____1/4 credit toward earning 5 minutes of "chat time" for the entire class at the end of the lesson. When you have collected four of these coupons, you can turn them in for a "chat time."

McEwan, E., & Damer, M. *Managing Unmanageable Students: Practical Solutions for Administrators.*
© 2000, Corwin Press, Inc.

EXHIBIT 4.1   Sample Coupon Packet

Provide Plenty of Pizzazz

The positive reinforcement must have enough pizzazz. Although increased praise will motivate most students to work harder, sometimes a teacher will have to use more ingenuity in planning effective reinforcements to use with the unmanageable student. One teacher created an elaborate fortune-teller's corner to excite her students about earning the cleverly worded fortunes they selected from a colorfully decorated jar. Another teacher awarded puzzle-shaped pieces of a camera; when students earned all six pieces forming a complete camera, they were given free time to shoot pictures around the school. One formerly irascible student worked hard all day to earn time to do stand-up comedy routines during the final 5 or 10 minutes of class.

Offer a Variety of Choices

The teacher should develop a list of several positive reinforcers from which the child can choose. If a teacher selects only one reinforcer, it is only a matter of time until the student is bored and no longer motivated by a single option. By developing a menu of possible reinforcers that can be written on a posted list or depicted in a coupon book, the teacher avoids the inevitable satiation that comes when one reward is repeatedly used. If a teacher tells you that reinforcement worked for 1 or 2 weeks before fizzling, satiation is most often the culprit. A reinforcer menu listing between 4 and 10 choices will not only provide variety but also enable the student to feel more control and ownership. The teacher might be setting the rules and consequences, but the student has the choice about reward.

Think Long-Range and Act Short-Term

Typical students can be motivated to work for long-range options, such as a future classroom field trip or a pizza party. If such options were successful with the unmanageable students in your school, they would not be so difficult. Such students would have responded to the natural long-range motivators that teachers typically use. Consider one possible explanation for the failure. John is still not following Ms. Gergovich's rules even though she implemented the "marbles in the jar" reinforcement program last month. The jar is not even filled to the halfway point and by now he has forgotten what she told him would happen when it was full. Meanwhile, Ms. Gergovich is so frustrated that the program is not working, she forgets to put the marbles in the jar most of the time.

Most unmanageable students need to earn a reinforcer choice at least twice a day, if not more often. These are students whose ability to wait for gratification is typically short, and although you will want to increase their ability to wait, when you are first resolving the behavior problems your primary goal is success. The younger the student, the more frequently he or she needs to earn a reinforcer choice. Jennifer, a middle school student who earns a point at the end of each class in which she has not sworn at the teacher, is capable of turning in her points for a coupon of her choice at the end of the day. Giselle, a first grader who leaves her desk and sometimes the classroom, might need to exchange her points for a reinforcer choice every 2 hours.

Remember the 80% Commandment

Whenever teachers design a plan where a student earns reinforcers, they should try to ensure that their students will earn the reinforcer choices 80% of the time. Because students quickly become frustrated and give up if they are unable to earn their reinforcement with 80% success, it is always preferable to start out with an easier plan that gradually becomes more difficult. Perhaps the teacher will only expect one improved behavior at first. Perhaps the teacher will begin the reinforcement plan by permitting the student to earn a reinforcer choice if he or she earns at least three of the six points that are possible to earn during the morning.

Use Premack Power

The Premack principle tells us, "First we do the activity we don't like as much, then we get to do the activity we like." When students have a difficult time looking beyond the immediate task that they find difficult or tedious, a teacher's conscious use of the Premack principle will help to move them past that hurdle. Many of our students with unmanageable behaviors do not sit through a difficult writing assignment or math lesson, strategically thinking that soon the dreaded activity will be finished and the class will move on to something else. Students with unmanageable behaviors become lost in the moment, and time seems endless. Unless the teacher reminds them or draws their attention to the schedule chart, these students are unlikely to remember that their favorite gym class begins in just 15 minutes and that a bit more effort will get them through the activity they dislike.

Ms. Schrock, who routinely Premacks in the classroom might tell her students, "If we complete the discussion on the digestive system, with everyone paying attention and remembering to raise a hand before talking, we'll have time to play the 'Jeopardy Food Groups Game.'" She knows that Todd and Misty are more likely to get off-task during the difficult discussion and question period, and she wants to focus them to the final game activity they enjoy. The teachers of our youth routinely employed the Premack principle whenever they said, "The row that is waiting quietly will line up first for lunch." Echoes of Premacking statements fill the halls of any school: "Finish the math paper and then you can either draw at your desk or read a book," "If you have worked quietly you will be allowed to write your answers on the board." Teachers who regularly interject these connections provide motivation when there is a learning task or waiting time with which the student with unmanageable behaviors has difficulty.

Reinforcer Pitfalls

Positive reinforcement has earned a bad reputation among educators because, like any good idea, it can backfire when misused. Knowing the most common reinforcement pitfalls will help you keep an eye open for situations in which teachers can actually cause more harm than good.

1. *School staff should avoid dispensing food as reinforcement whenever possible.* We find it hard to quibble with educators' charges of bribery when a teacher dispenses candy or soda as reinforcement. With rising concerns about students' penchants for instant drug highs and an increase in food disorders, the teacher who relies on the quick-fix sugar rush of junk food is justifiably open to criticism. Dispensing food is easy and takes little preplanning or thought, but watching a teacher dole out the food reminds everyone involved of those old Skinnerian pigeon-training movies. Teachers who take this route use little creativity in determining what motivates their difficult students. Some principals avoid this issue by not allowing food reinforcement unless the school team has agreed to waive the standing policy for a specific student. If you decide on this course of action, provide your teachers with lists of creative reinforcers. Keep a collection of resource books in the teachers' lounge. See Appendix B for a list of helpful books and kits for teachers. Ask staff members who routinely use creative reinforcers to describe them at staff meetings.

2. *Always keep your staff focused on the goal of fading out the most overt types of reinforcement.* Even though Cherise earned points for daily coupons in fourth grade, by the beginning of fifth grade she was working for once-a-week reinforcement, and by sixth grade her point program was successfully discontinued. Although the student with unmanageable behaviors does not start out with the necessary self-control or intrinsic motivation to follow the rules, the goal is always to develop those two characteristics.

We suggest that teachers plan from the outset about how they can make their behavior intervention more challenging as the student begins to achieve success. Only if the teacher sets increasingly higher expectations will he or she wean the student away from the more contrived reinforcers used in the beginning.

3. *Positive reinforcers should never be the only strategy used with unmanageable students.* If a teacher violates the 80% commandment, if clear rules have not been established and consistently followed, or if a distractible student has to complete independent work sitting in a pod of six students, the root causes of the unmanageable behavior have still not been addressed. Positive reinforcement should, however, always accompany any environmental, curricular, or instructional changes.

The Dreaded "Criticism Trap"

You can easily determine how effectively a classroom teacher is positively reinforcing the unmanageable student or the entire classroom by using the Reinforcement Analysis Form (Form 4.1) to collect frequency data. This information will let you know how often the teacher is praising or complimenting in contrast to correcting or criticizing. Once the data has been collected, you can analyze whether a criticism trap is in operation with all of the students in the classroom or only with the child presenting problems, whether the teacher uses enough reinforcement, and whether the teacher's verbal reinforcement specifically describes the behavior that the teacher wants to acknowledge.

The person collecting the reinforcement data should sit on the sidelines with the Reinforcement Analysis Form, making a check mark each time the teacher either reinforces/compliments or corrects/criticizes either the entire class or an individual student. If the person taking data circles the check mark when comments or actions are directed exclusively to the student with unmanageable behaviors, then it is possible to differentiate the teacher's level of reinforcement to the class from the level used with a student such as Louie whose noncompliance in class has led to a team staffing. If Louie's teacher says, "Katie's group is doing a good job of being quiet," the observer will put a check mark on the top half of the form. If the teacher later says, "Great answer Louie" the data taker will put another check mark on the top half of the form, circling the mark because it was directed to Louie. In contrast, if the teacher says, "Go back to your seat now. You are supposed to be working, Louie," the observer will put a circled check mark on the bottom half of the form. If the teacher corrects a word that another child is reading and says, "No, that word is *big*," the observer will put another check mark on the bottom half of the form. For the entire 20 or 30 minutes, the observer will note all of the teacher's reinforcing or corrective-negative feedback. Exhibit 4.2 shows what data looks like when a teacher is using praise effectively.

The definitions on the Reinforcement Analysis Form (Form 4.1), should help the observer decide in which of the two categories the check mark should go: (a) reinforcing feedback, or (b) corrective-negative feedback. Reinforcing feedback includes any type of verbal or nonverbal approval that is given to one child or to a group of children. The teacher is

Student: _____   Teacher: _____
Date: _____   Start Time: _____
Setting: _____   Stop Time: _____
Activity: _____
Observer: _____

Directions: Each time the teacher exhibits the behavior, make a check mark in a square. Samples of specific
feedback can be recorded underneath the appropriate section.

R												

Reinforcing Feedback:
Teacher praises, gives a point or reward, physically shows approval for a correct response/appropriate
behavior, or makes a positive comment in response to a correct answer, good effort, or appropriate behavior.
In order to count a praise statement as reinforcing, the physical behavior of the teacher must be clearly
positive: verbal approval should be accompanied either by a change of facial expression or voice.

CN												

Corrective-Negative Feedback
Teacher makes negative statements or disciplinary comments, punishes, points at the student, or otherwise
shows disapproval for incorrect answers, responses, or inappropriate behaviors. This feedback includes any
warning from the teacher after the student incorrectly answers, incorrectly responds, or inappropriately
behaves. Warnings include verbal warnings, "shh" reminders, and check mark warnings put on the board. If
the teacher tells students the rules *before* they break them in order to avoid inappropriate behavior, this action
does not count as corrective-negative feedback. For example, if the teacher says, "Remember to walk quietly
in the hallway" before the students walk in the hallway, do not count a tally mark.

Reinforcing Feedback/Minutes _____ / _____ = _____ Reinforcing Responses Per Minute.

Ratio of Reinforcing Feedback: Corrective-Negative Feedback _____ : _____

McEwan, E., & Damer, M. *Managing Unmanageable Students: Practical Solutions for Administrators.*
© 2000, Corwin Press, Inc.

FORM 4.1 Reinforcement Analysis Form

Student: **Entire Class**   Teacher: **Ms. Munez**
Date: **4/7**   Start Time: **1:30**
Setting: **Language Arts**   Stop Time: **1:45**
Activity: **Group Work/Discussion**
Observer: **Marion Metlzer**

Directions: Each time the teacher exhibits the behavior, make a check mark in a square. Samples of specific feedback can be recorded underneath the appropriate section.

√	√	√	√	√	√	√	√	√	√	√	√	√	
R														

Reinforcing Feedback
Teacher praises, gives a point or reward, physically shows approval for a correct response or appropriate behavior, or makes a positive comment in response to a correct answer, good effort, or appropriate behavior. In order to count a praise statement as reinforcing, the physical behavior of the teacher must be clearly positive: verbal approval should be accompanied by a change of either facial expression or voice.

Good choice.	**Your hand was up so fast.**	**Everyone answered all 10 questions.**	**Yes, you've got it.**
Excellent!	**Good example.**	**You remembered the rule.**	**Good sentence.**
Thumbs up.	**Your paper looks good.**	**First day that everybody knew that answer.**	
Nice work.		**Clever!**	

√	√	√											
CN														

Corrective-Negative Feedback
Teacher makes negative statements or disciplinary comments, punishes, points at the student, or otherwise shows disapproval for incorrect answers, responses, or inappropriate behaviors. This feedback includes any warning from the teacher after the student incorrectly answers, incorrectly responds, or inappropriately behaves. Warnings include verbal warnings, "shh" reminders, and checkmark warnings put on the board. If the teacher tells students the rules *before* they break them in order to avoid inappropriate behavior, this action does not count as corrective-negative feedback. For example, if the teacher says, "Remember to walk quietly in the hallway" before the students walk in the hallway, do not count a tally mark.

Cherise, let's get back to work.   **John, you don't need to spend time doing that.**
Shh, remember to whisper when you talk to each other.

\# Reinforcing Feedback/Minutes   **13 / 15 min.** =   **.87** Reinforcing Responses Per Minute
Ratio of Reinforcing Feedback: Corrective-Negative Feedback **13 : 3** or approximately **4 : 1**

McEwan, E., & Damer, M. *Managing Unmanageable Students: Practical Solutions for Administrators.*
© 2000, Corwin Press, Inc.

EXHIBIT 4.2 Completed Reinforcement Analysis Form: The Use of Effective Praise

providing reinforcing feedback whenever he or she praises, claps his or her hands in appreciation, gives a point or reward, physically shows approval for a correct response or for appropriate behavior, or makes a positive statement or appreciative comment in response to a correct answer, good effort, or appropriate behavior. To count a praise statement as reinforcing, the physical behavior of the teacher must be clearly positive to the child. For example, if the teacher says, "Okay" or "Yes" in a bland tone of voice and with no accompanying smile, this neutral feedback is not considered a positive stroke. Make only one check mark for an uninterrupted string of several positive sentences such as, "Super job, Rachel. I think you are doing your best cutting today. You must have eaten a great breakfast."

Corrective-negative feedback includes any time that the teacher admonishes, makes negative statements or disciplinary comments, punishes, points at the student, or otherwise verbally or nonverbally shows disapproval for incorrect answers, responses, or inappropriate behaviors. This feedback also includes any type of warnings from the teacher for incorrect answers, incorrect responses, or inappropriate behaviors. Warnings include verbal warnings, "shh" reminders, and check mark warnings put on the board. If the teacher tells the children the rules before they break them in order to avoid inappropriate behavior, this does not count as corrective-negative feedback. For example, if the teacher says, "Remember to walk quietly in the hallway," before the students walk in the hallway, do not make a check mark. If, while the students are walking in the hallway, one child pushes another child and the teacher says, "Louie, don't push. Come here," make a check mark and circle it. If the teacher says, "This class is too noisy. I can't think," make another check mark.

Once the data has been collected, count the total number of check marks recorded for the top half of the page, count the total number of check marks on the bottom half, and determine the ratio. In a well-run classroom environment where optimal learning is occurring, your data will show that the teacher makes three or four reinforcing statements for every negative statement. The younger the students or the more difficult the work, the higher this ratio should be. When this 3:1 ratio is reversed, the classroom teacher may be locked into a criticism trap. Such a teacher routinely "shushes" or corrects students' behaviors because that critical response seems to work. After the teacher gives the negative consequence, typically the student gets back to work or stops the misbehavior for a few moments. Although the teacher perceives the negative consequence as effective, he or she has been fooled because the misbehavior soon resumes. In a class where a criticism trap is operating, the students primarily receive attention by misbehaving. Many times you will see a criticism trap pattern when teachers take Kohn so literally that they are afraid to compliment students' good work. Sometimes a teacher who is locked into a criticism trap has never learned to praise children effortlessly. Conditions are ripe for the criticism trap when the following take place:

1. The students are working at frustration levels and their accuracy dips below 80%.

2. The students are seated in very close proximity to one another.

3. The classroom is chaotic and the rules are not followed consistently.

In situations where the ratio of reinforcing feedback to critical-negative feedback is 1:3, the teacher's attention is increasingly snagged by the escalating misbehavior. Whether watching an out-of-control kindergarten classroom or a disruptive middle school social studies lesson, you can observe as many as 10 critical-negative teacher comments for every reinforcing one. Exhibit 4.3 shows data taken in a room where a teacher is caught in a criticism trap.

Teachers locked into criticism traps are exhausted by the end of May. Their stress and tension levels skyrocket as misbehavior escalates. When a criticism trap is occurring, the students' behavior will predictably continue to deteriorate unless the teacher changes his or her behavior and makes the necessary environmental changes. Any teacher of a student with unmanageable behaviors has compounded problems when a criticism trap with the entire classroom takes hold. Unless such a teacher can conduct the larger classroom with more effective management, the likelihood of helping resolve a single student's unmanageable behaviors is slim.

In our combined years of observing, we find that in a well-run kindergarten, first-, or second-grade classroom, during most activities the teacher will give the children reinforcing feedback at least once every 1 or 2 minutes. If middle and high school students are routinely on-task, effective teachers will provide reinforcing feedback every 5 minutes during most activities. To compute the class rate-per-minute after the data is collected, divide the total number of all reinforcing feedback occurrences by the number of minutes you observed. If the teacher gave four reinforcing comments or actions in 20 minutes, divide 4 by 20 to get .2 rate-per-minute, which tells you that the teacher needs to provide more reinforcement.

When teachers are told that they should be positive once every minute or two, they blanch in horror and insist that this would interfere with teaching. One of the authors heard this skepticism so often that she finally made a videotape of a superior middle school teacher maintaining this high rate of reinforcement throughout a delightful language arts lesson comprised of reading, discussion, and writing activities. When teachers watched the videotape and used the Reinforcement Analysis Form to analyze instruction, they were surprised to discover that throughout the students' animated discussion of Icarus and his father, the teacher in the videotape was naturally praising through words and gestures. This master teacher made the process look effortless and "normal." If you are fortunate to have such a teacher on your staff, videotape a typical lesson and

Student: **Entire Class**   Teacher: **Mr. Wright**
Date: **5/4**   Start Time: **9:10**
Setting: **Math Class (large group)**   Stop Time: **9: 30**
Activity: **Discussion/ board work/independent**
Observer: **Lee Sykuta**

Directions: Each time the teacher exhibits the behavior, make a check mark in a square. Samples of specific
           feedback can be recorded underneath the appropriate section.

√	√	√												

R

Reinforcing Feedback
Teacher praises, gives a point or reward, physically shows approval for a correct response/appropriate
behavior, or makes a positive comment in response to a correct answer, good effort, or appropriate behavior.
In order to count a praise statement as reinforcing, the physical behavior of the teacher must be clearly
positive: verbal approval should be accompanied either by a change of facial expression or voice.

> **Great answer.**
> **Nice thought you put in solving that problem.**
> **I like the way Row #1 is working.**

√	√	√	√	√	√	√	√	√	√	√				

CN

Corrective-Negative Feedback
Teacher makes negative statements or disciplinary comments, punishes, points at the student, or otherwise
shows disapproval for incorrect answers, responses, or inappropriate behaviors. This feedback includes any
warning from the teacher after the student incorrectly answers, incorrectly responds, or inappropriately
behaves. Warnings include verbal warnings, "shh" reminders, and check mark warnings put on the board. If
the teacher tells the children the rules *before* they break them in order to avoid inappropriate behavior, this
action does not count as corrective-negative feedback. For example, if the teacher says, "Remember to walk
quietly in the hallway" before the students walk in the hallway, do not make a check mark.

Give yourself a warning check.	**Put that away; this is math class.**	**You just take care of Angie.**
Shh, quiet.	**You shouldn't be talking.**	**Jason, sit down right now.**
You need to turn around.	**You are out of your space.**	**No (head shake).**
Shh, I can't hear.	**People, this isn't fourth grade behavior.**	

Reinforcing Feedback/Minutes   **3 / 20 min.**   =   **.15** Reinforcing Responses Per Minute.

Ratio of Reinforcing Feedback: Corrective-Negative Feedback   **3: 11 or   approx. 1: 4**

McEwan, E., & Damer, M. *Managing Unmanageable Students: Practical Solutions for Administrators.*
© 2000, Corwin Press, Inc.

EXHIBIT 4.3   Completed Reinforcement Analysis Form: The Criticism Trap

teach your staff to take reinforcement data on the tape. Until they see this teaching behavior effectively used, they will remain skeptical.

As data is taken on reinforcement, write the exact teacher comments in the space provided below the definitions. A sarcastic teacher or a phony praiser who keeps saying blandly, "Good job" will be shocked when confronted with this matter-of-fact data.

After you have looked at the classroom reinforcement rate, compare it to the type of feedback the student with unmanageable behaviors receives. Is the teacher locked into a criticism trap with this student? Does the teacher provide feedback only on the student's misbehaviors? Does the student receive very little feedback that is either positive or negative, as the teacher ignores all but the most egregious offenses? The student with unmanageable behaviors who typically receives more critical/corrective feedback because of higher levels of misbehavior also needs to receive more reinforcing feedback to ensure the 3:1 ratio that is necessary for a change in behavior. When data show that the teacher is locked into a criticism trap with the student, recommend that your team help the teacher design a reinforcement plan. More punishment will only increase the already overwhelming amount of criticism coming at the student.

Developing a Plan That Uses Reinforcement Effectively

"Greg is so difficult, it's hard to praise him." "I have so many things to think about, how could I ever bring a reinforcement plan into this classroom." Whenever the teacher of an unmanageable student needs to increase positive reinforcement but is balking, or when your staff wants to use a point program, always suggest a Differential Reinforcement of Omission of Behavior (DRO) plan, the most powerful reinforcement plan available. A DRO plan enables the teacher to award points to a student at intervals of time in which the unmanageable behavior does not happen. The DRO plan helps the teacher to encourage more desirable behavior at the same time he or she provides feedback on the unmanageable behavior.

Let's look at the DRO plan developed for Greg, a fourth-grade student, whose outright refusal to follow the teacher's instruction combined with impulsive, in-your-face behavior with other students in the class has frustrated his teacher all year. The principal and team members at Cranston School completed Steps 1 through 3 on the Behavior Intervention Planning Form provided in Chapter 2 and decided to develop a DRO reinforcement plan. In order to plan the DRO, they referred to their data to see how often Greg's disruptive behavior was occurring. The data helped them to determine whether they would start with smaller or longer inter-

Time	Point
8:00-8:30	
8:30-9:05	
9:05-9:35	
9:35-10:15	
10:15-10:45	
10:45-11:15	
11:15-11:45	
11:45-12:15	
12:15-12:45	
12:45-1:20	
1:20-1:50	
1:50-2:25	
2:25 Exchange Time 9 out of 12 points needed for exchange	Total Daily Points = _____

McEwan, E., & Damer, M. *Managing Unmanageable Students: Practical Solutions for Administrators.*
© 2000, Corwin Press, Inc.

EXHIBIT 4.4   Greg's Data Collection Form

vals. They also needed to determine how many times each day Greg should receive a reinforcer exchange for the points he has earned. In Exhibit 4.4, Greg could earn points at intervals set at approximately every 30 minutes with one reward exchange each day. Interval times varied so that they would match the teacher's class schedule. Each behavior management plan will require its own unique data collection form dictated by the teacher's schedule, the length of interval, and the exchange ratio.

Although Greg could potentially earn 12 points each day, he needed only 9 for a reinforcer exchange. The staff wanted to make sure that he earned 80% of his points each day before gradually requiring that he earn 10 or more.

Our experience shows that if intervals of less than 20 minutes are used, then the classroom teacher needs another adult in the classroom to assist with the DRO behavior plan. If the intervals are 20 minutes or longer, the classroom teacher armed with a relatively quiet timer or an athletic watch and a clipboard can use the DRO plan independently.

Although the variations on this basic DRO plan are limitless, begin with a basic plan similar to Greg's. You can develop your own unique DRO plans as you become more skillful.

Greg's Reinforcement Plan: DRO

Student: Greg Majercz

Date: 2/09/99

Teacher: Jayne Matthews

School: Cranston Meadows

Problem behaviors: Disturbing others with hands, feet, and/or objects. Noncompliance with teacher's requests and directions.

Behavior Objectives

1. To increase Greg's ability to respect other people: keep his hands, feet, and other objects to himself. Greg is keeping his hands and feet to himself when he is not pushing, tripping, touching, poking, grabbing someone's pencil, writing on another student's paper, or engaging in any similar behavior to another student or person in the school environment. This includes engaging in these behaviors with hands, arms, feet, or any objects.

2. To increase Greg's ability to follow the teacher's directions. Greg is compliant when he is following the teacher's instructions and directions. If the teacher asks him to line up with the other children, Greg will line up. If he is being noisy in line and the teacher reminds him to use a quiet voice, he will begin to use a quiet voice. If he is bopping his pencil on his desk and the teacher asks him to stop, he will put the pencil down within a few moments.

Positive Reinforcement

Greg will have the opportunity to earn a point at the end of every interval during the course of the school day. At the end of every interval, the teacher will briefly praise him if he has earned his points and then record the points on Greg's Data Collection Form, Exhibit 4.4, shown earlier.

If Greg has not earned his point, the teacher will describe in a quiet, informational tone of voice why the point was not earned. Greg will automatically earn a point if he has fulfilled the target behavior requirements by (a) respecting other people by keeping his hands, feet, and other objects to self, and (b) following the teacher's directions.

If Greg has not kept his hands, feet, or other objects to himself, or has not followed the teacher's instructions and directions, he will not earn his point for the interval. The classroom teacher must have seen Greg engage in the inappropriate behavior for it to affect the point total. If another child tattles on Greg, but the teacher has not seen the behavior, it will not result in a point loss.

The teacher will continue to record whether Greg earned a point or did not at the end of each interval until the time in the day when he can exchange his points for an item or activity from the reinforcer menu.

Praise will continue to be delivered by the teacher intermittently throughout the intervals for appropriate behaviors (in seat, following teacher's instructions, independent working, showing self-control, respecting property) and academic behaviors (task-oriented, completion of task, correct answer, imaginative answer).

Reinforcers

The classroom teacher will select a list of approximately eight items for inclusion on the reinforcement menu. Some items that will be included are the following:

1. Earning a pass to use the computer in the learning center
2. Earning the opportunity to read a video magazine in the learning center
3. Earning the opportunity to design a worksheet for another student
4. Earning the opportunity to help in the kindergarten class

This behavior program will only succeed if Greg desires the items on the reinforcer menu. Some days the teacher might want to add a novel option. If a reinforcer is never selected by Greg, replace it with another item. Sometimes the silliest ideas become the best reinforcers. Greg might enjoy earning the opportunity to tell a few jokes to the class or to sit with the teacher after school and describe his Star Wars cards.

In addition to the reinforcement at exchange time, Greg will keep an ongoing record of his daily point total in a teacher-constructed bankbook. Another reinforcer list will be developed for this grand point total. Maintaining a grand point total will serve to motivate Greg when he has lost too many points by 12:00 for an exchange that day. The teacher can remind

Greg that the points he earns still count for the big item. Greg's reinforcement menu for the grand point total will include:

150 points: Opportunity to shoot baskets with the principal

150 points: McDonald's lunch delivered to him at lunchtime

150 points: Trip to Magic Waters Park with parents

Implementation Guidelines

The classroom teacher should maintain consistency in awarding points at the end of each interval. If the teacher finds this difficult, a timer or athletic watch can help the teacher remember.

Greg should not receive warnings or threats about a point loss. Greg has either earned or not earned points. If the rules are not clearly followed, the message to him is unclear and there is always the chance that a behavior will be overlooked.

Feedback at the end of the interval should be specific about why the point was or was not earned.

Staff Coordination Roles

1. Ms. Matthews will design daily point sheets and will adapt a weekly data sheet for accountability.

2. Ms. Matthews will develop a written classroom chart with the two behavior rules listed.

3. Ms. Matthews and the principal will design the reinforcement menus (daily ones and the long-term one).

4. Ms. Matthews will explain the behavior system to Greg and the class and will notify Greg's parents about the new motivational system before she begins using it.

5. This program will begin on 2/18.

Issues for Staff Members to Explore During Team Meetings

1. Is Greg's success rate around a minimum of 80%? If not, what adjustments can be made?

2. Do target definitions (e.g., keeping hands, feet, and objects to himself) need more specification for consistency?

3. When will the teacher decide that Greg's point level can be increased to 10/12 points for an exchange? Is he ready to move to longer intervals? These changes should be the next two steps.

4. Are the reinforcers motivating for Greg? Does the teacher sometimes add a surprise reinforcer to the menu?

5. What roadblocks to successful implementation did the team overlook?

The behavior consultant who worked with the teachers to design Greg's DRO plan did not think that the odds were in favor of success. Because the principal's position was split between two buildings, she was always on the run, never in one spot for more than a minute or two. After hiring the behavior consultant, she remained out of the picture, and the success or failure of the plan rested with a somewhat resistant teacher who was outspoken about her skepticism that the DRO was worth the time and energy. After the teacher finalized the plan, the behavior consultant never again heard from the school site and assumed that Greg had continued to frustrate the staff.

This story did have happy ending. Two years later, the behavior consultant was teaching her first day of a discipline and classroom management course for K-12 educators. After introducing the concept of a DRO, the behavior consultant found herself addressing concerns raised by the teachers. The teachers protested that no teacher could teach and use a DRO for one student at the same time. The teachers were convinced that the other students would resent a troublemaker getting all this attention. When the behavior consultant called on a teacher whose hand was vigorously waving in the air, she recognized the woman who had been Greg's teacher.

"Let me describe how this can work," Greg's former teacher began explaining before describing the positive changes in Greg after she began to use the plan. "The first week was confusing and I didn't know if I was going to stop the plan or what," she described. "Greg soon knew exactly when it was time for his points, so I didn't even need the timer, and I found that I no longer had to spend all of my time correcting his behavior or wondering what would come next." By the end of the year, she had been able to increase the time intervals, and although she still described Greg as "challenging," she no longer wanted to go home and quit teaching every evening. Her infomercial on the benefits of DRO plans positively impacted the other teachers' opinions as nothing else could have and the behavior consultant wished she could videotape this teacher's recommendation to be shown in every class she taught.

As you can tell from Greg's story, rewards can be powerful reinforcers and motivators for behavior change. But they will not work in every situation. You and your team will also benefit from a thorough understanding of punishment and how to make it work for you. You will find everything you need to know in Chapter 5.

CHAPTER FIVE

Punishment

What It Is and How to Make It Work for You

The subject of punishment is emotion laden and confusing. One group of educators believes that all responses to students should be positive and supportive; that no students should be criticized or reprimanded in any way in order not to crush their self-esteem or internal motivation. The other group sanctions the use of punishment, or what they believe to be punishment, and attempt to impose it in a rational manner—consistently, fairly, and with clear objectives.

In response to the first group, we believe that genuine punishment is a necessary and effective tool for correcting unacceptable behavior and that educators who malign punishment are naïve. In response to the second group, we would argue that many educators who punish are not really punishing at all. They may be trying to achieve retribution for some wronged victim or to bring about corrective behavior, or perhaps they are venting their frustrations or even indulging in a bit of vengeance. But often they are not carrying out genuine *punishment*, which we define strictly as any punitive consequence that brings about a reduction in the frequency or the severity of a behavior.

Although we respect the cautions and limitations associated with punishment, we still believe that when used appropriately, punishment remains an effective tool for managing unmanageable students. We are not talking about corporal punishment or imprisonment in stocks on the school commons, but about consequences that if used judiciously and with careful planning can make your school a more hospitable and secure place in which to study and work.

Punishments and How They Work

When Is a Punishment Not a Punishment?

Consider the punitive value of the following responses to student misbehavior.

1. Ms. Angelitis, Marta's teacher, punishes her for not completing work by making her stay in at recess. Marta has missed at least two recesses each week all year.

2. Mikell's teacher, Mr. Brown, punishes him for coming late to class or being unprepared by deducting five points from his grade. Mikell has maintained an "F" this semester.

3. Ms. Alderman, Holly's teacher, punishes her by giving her blue slips for shouting and pushing in the halls. Because three blue slips result in an all day in-school suspension, Holly has consistently missed class at least once every other week.

Although all three teachers believe they are punishing the students' behaviors, the punitive procedures they chose ultimately had no impact. In the book, *Discipline in the Secondary Classroom: A Problem-by-Problem Survival Guide,* Randall Sprick (1985) offers a definition of *punishment* that helps explain the misunderstanding that many educators have with the term:

> A consequence is only a punishment if it reduces the future frequency of a behavior. Grounding a child is a punishment only if it reduces how often the misbehavior later takes place. A punishment can be something the teacher does or says. It can be something other students do or say, or a punishment can be something the student thinks or feels himself. Punishments are not necessarily overt consequences such as time out, suspension, or some form of corporal punishment. A punishment is anything that results in a behavior taking place less and less often in the future. If a consequence does not reduce the future frequency of a behavior, it is not a punishment. (p. 92)

We have found that this view of punishment helps us to make decisions more effectively and evaluate student situations in which punishment is used or being considered. Although in other situations the three consequences listed above (loss of a recess privilege, point deduction, and in-school suspension) might be punishments, in these examples they were a waste of time and effort for their teachers because they did not lead to the desired results.

The list of potential punishments is so extensive that even teachers who cringe at the word, preferring to view themselves as warm fuzzy types, routinely punish. Any one of these consequences is a punishment if its effect over time is to reduce or eliminate a student's behavior.

1. Verbal correction or reprimand (corrective-negative feedback)
2. Warning after student does the behavior or "shushing"
3. Loss of privilege
4. Owing time
5. Loss of a responsibility
6. Phone call to parent
7. Point deduction or lowered grade
8. Confiscation
9. Natural consequence after spilling, tearing, dirtying, or throwing something
10. Extra work, writing, or exercise
11. Referral to the principal
12. Any type of time-out away from the group, out of the classroom, or in a special area
13. In-school suspension
14. Detention after school

Why Punish?

We use punishment for some very good reasons. It can rapidly stop behavior. When a toddler repeatedly runs out into a busy street, even after heart-to-heart chats about the inherent dangers, we pick him up, paddle his bottom, and hope we have eliminated this highly dangerous behavior.

When paired with instruction, punishment provides helpful feedback to students by teaching a lesson in a dramatic and, one hopes, never-to-be-forgotten format. Sometimes punishment can even be a deterrent to peers. When reasoning, clear instruction, and other approaches have failed, sometimes nothing works quite as effectively as creative and timely punishment.

The Principal's Role in Punishing Students

As a principal, you have more hands-on involvement in consequences intended as punishments than for any other type of intervention. Juanita was referred to your office yesterday for swearing at a teacher. Corrine skipped school to ride the train into the city. William was throwing food in the cafeteria, and the toilets are plugged up because Arturo stuffed them with paper towels. Because you are directly involved in all of these situations, as well as responsible for seeing that related ethical and legal considerations for punishment procedures are followed in your school, you need to thoroughly understand punishment guidelines, pitfalls, and the latest federal and state laws. Best practices dictate that teachers and schools should always select the least restrictive punishment for students. Anytime a punishment consequence adversely affects student learning or when extremely negative behaviors can arise as a result of its use, then the punishment is considered as restrictive. If Manuel falls farther behind in his schoolwork after 3 days of in-school suspension, the school team should investigate whether other punishment alternatives that keep him in the classroom would convince him to stop throwing food in the cafeteria. Losing the right to sit with his buddies for a week would not affect his schoolwork and would probably be more effective.

If your school district is still relying on suspensions and detentions as the mainstay of its discipline policy, follow the advice of Johns, Carr, and Hoots (1997):

> In this time of increasing violence and increasing complaints and lawsuits against school districts over suspensions and expulsion, it is critical that all districts develop acceptable alternative methods of discipline. Such methods will result not only in a safer and more productive school environment, but in dollar savings in legal proceedings. (p. 11)

Organize a district committee to develop a list of consequences for disruptive student behavior that includes alternatives to the most restrictive punishments. Because punishment only suppresses a behavior and does not teach more acceptable alternatives, make sure you avoid a discipline plan that lists only punishment strategies.

Punishment Guidelines

Be sure to keep the following guidelines in mind when developing your intervention plan.

Always Provide Specific Verbal Feedback

Punishment should be informative. The person who is giving the punishment (articulating the reprimand, taking away the point, telling the student to go to the office) should always tell the student firmly but unemotionally, why he or she is receiving it.

The tone of voice should be assertive but not aggressive. Loud reprimands can actually increase disruptive behaviors in comparison to soft reprimands, which are more effective (Paine, Darch, Deutchman, Radicchi, & Rosellini, 1983). Corrective feedback to a student should identify the misbehavior as descriptively as possible and inform the student of how the misbehavior affects the other students or staff. If a posted rule has been broken, the student's attention should be focused to the rule. Finally, the punisher should either describe what the student should be doing or describe the punishment consequence and why it has been chosen. Two examples of informative verbal feedback are the following:

1. "When you throw food, it can hit another student and the custodians have to clean up the mess. The cafeteria rules are posted over the door. I want you to wait here until the other students leave. You have a week of sitting at Mr. Grisby's table. It's the rule."

2. "When you walk over to Gretta's desk and draw on her paper, she can't concentrate on her work. Our class rules say we should keep our hands to ourselves which means on our own property. I would like you to go back to your desk and start writing the caterpillar story."

Be Sure You Are Not Encouraging Misbehavior

If Lynette wants to escape the classroom because the work is too difficult, one of the other students is harassing her, or she has a personality clash with the teacher, then a teacher who punishes her noncompliance by sending her out of the room is actually reinforcing her. By the end of next month, Lynette will be predictably noncompliant more often than she is today. When a student's misbehavior increases, always check out whether negative reinforcement can explain the rise.

Never Use Punishment Without Reinforcement

"The most powerful treatment available for changing the behavior of acting-out children in school settings consists of a combination of positive reinforcement procedures and mild punishment" (Walker, 1979, p. 31).

Because punishment does not teach a student how to behave more acceptably, it should never be used alone. A teacher who uses verbal reprimands to stop students from blurting out answers in class will reach his or her goal more quickly by also teaching the rule for hand raising at the beginning of the year and praising students who raise their hands. Principals who have established a punishment policy that students who scream at the lunch table must sit away from friends for 2 days will have a quieter lunchroom if they have also developed an incentive program to reward classes that follow the rules. Classes in which students follow the lunchroom rules can have the opportunity to earn the privilege of entering the lunch line first.

Plan Ahead

Students are less likely to respond explosively to punishment when rules have been explained in advance and when they see that those rules are followed consistently and fairly. Ask the teachers on your staff to list their punishment strategies and to clearly describe when they use them. Students in the classroom should not have to guess whether Mr. Knight would keep a student after class during the passing period. The rules and consequences he has explained and posted should unequivocally tell them. Likewise, the rules and consequences should be clearly spelled out for your school so that you can explain them to the students, teachers, and parents in advance. What is the consequence for pushing and yelling on the bus? What happens when a student purposely floods the bathroom toilets?

Once punishment consequences have been determined, they need to be followed consistently. If students are sometimes punished for pushing and yelling on the bus and other times ignored, they will continue their rowdy behavior. Many students will opt to take a chance and loudly yell on the bus or throw a pencil in class if they think they are likely to get away with it.

Avoid Public Punishment

When Grayson is punished in front of his peers, they will either shun or ridicule him, or feel increased support and sympathy. All of these outcomes put the teacher in a no-win situation. If Grayson thinks that the teacher has humiliated him in front of his peers ("dissed" him in today's dialect), he will be more likely to act out and possibly escalate into an overt confrontation, especially if he is in middle or high school. In contrast, if Grayson is perceived as a martyr and receives peer sympathy, his original misbehavior may escalate because of his peer's attention.

Although we recognize that it is not always possible to take the student to the side of the room or to a less public location, school staff should always try to avoid the problems caused by public punishment. After verbal feedback has failed to stop Ronnie from disrupting the class with his clowning antics, Ms. Miglio might ask him to see her before he leaves the classroom. After the other students have left, she can privately tell Ronnie that he will lose 3 minutes of passing time in the hall. By talking to Ronnie privately, Ms. Miglio avoids risking an escalation of disruptive behavior as Ronnie tries to save face in front of his peers.

Be Sure to Follow Legal Guidelines and Restrictions for Students With IEPs

Following the latest mandates regarding punishment for students who have special education classification can be so confusing that you will want to rely on your special education director to stay current on changes in the Individuals With Disabilities Education Act (IDEA; 1997). Use your school psychologist and school attorney as resources to provide you with the latest legal and ethical guidelines for use of punishment strategies such as a time-out. Always document any new behavior interventions in the IEP. If you have followed the steps in the Behavior Intervention Planning Form (Form 2.1), you will have established most of the necessary groundwork to take further steps if the student's behavior remains unmanageable. If you follow the recommended problem-solving process, you will meet IDEA requirements to complete a functional behavioral assessment, make necessary changes in the environment, and implement positive alternatives that are required as part of any disciplinary plan.

Punishment Pitfalls

When punishment is misused or overused, it can impair a student's learning, trigger depression, escalate into an overt confrontation, or worse. If you know the most common punishment pitfalls, you can avoid ethical and legal nightmares.

Frequent Punishment Lowers Self-Esteem

A student who is repeatedly punished can feel rejected and withdraw as a direct result of the punishment. Subsequently, the student may feign sickness, stop talking in school, cut classes, and ultimately drop out of school. When members of a school team notice these red flag signals in a student, they should use punishment only as a last resort, making sure that reinforcement levels stay high. School staff should always design a DRO program (reinforcement option) first rather than a punishment consequence with a student who appears susceptible to withdrawal or depression. Referrals to counseling should be made for students who fall into this category.

Too Much Punishment Will Backfire

Complain, complain, complain! If you have ever lived or worked with a nagger, you know how quickly you can learn to tune out that person. Soon you are oblivious to the barrage of complaints. Whether the punishment is negative-critical feedback, a phone call to parents, detention, or losing the privilege to have recess, it is only effective when misbehavior is successfully suppressed. Just as students will tune out the harangues of a nagging teacher, they will also become oblivious to repeated phone calls to their parents, lost recesses, and endless days of in-school suspensions. Whenever you see your staff members repeatedly doling out the same punishments like a broken record, help them change their approach. They are wasting their time.

A phone call to Gretchen's parents after she pushes another child at recess is an effective punishment if her teacher only has to use that consequence once or twice. If the teacher finds that weekly calls to Gretchen's parents are necessary because Gretchen still shoves and pushes other children every few days, then there is no reason to use that punishment. Gretchen is accustomed to losing recess.

Avoid the Punishment → Acceleration of Aggression/Agitation Chain

If you reflect on how you felt the last time a police officer gave you a speeding ticket, you can conjure up the anger that punishment can trigger. A small percentage of the students in your school will react to punishment with excessive anger. These are the students whose misbehavior predictably escalates the moment the teacher first gives them a warning check on the blackboard. Bob Waller, a rural principal, called in a behavior consultant because he was convinced that Tyrone, a middle school student in his school should be transferred to the alternative behavior disorders program as soon as possible. The parents had resisted the change in school placement leaving Mr. Waller desperate for another solution. One week earlier, Tyrone had leaped into the principal's chair and held the telephone in his lap threatening anyone who attempted to take it from him. Only after the police arrived was the situation resolved. Because Mr. Waller could not transfer the student, he now wanted assurance that Tyrone would not explode again.

A look back at that day's events provides a clear example of how a punishment → acceleration of aggression/agitation chain can rapidly escalate. Because an assertive discipline system was used in the classroom, whenever a student was not following one of the rules the teacher gave him or her a warning check on the blackboard. The teacher tried to catch each infraction, but in a class of 30 students, that was not always possible. Three checks affected the student's grade and resulted in a referral to the office. The teacher did not have a reinforcement plan to accompany this punishment system, and only infrequently praised students for correct answers.

After the teacher gave Tyrone his first warning check for not writing in his journal, Tyrone, who had a tendency to obsess over the smallest things, could not stop thinking about that check. His body tensed, his hands clenched, and he was unable to think of anything else. When the teacher gave him a second warning check for not working, Tyrone blurted out what he thought about her checks. A resulting third check from the teacher with instructions to march down to the office propelled Tyrone into even higher levels of anger. The principal quickly rushed to the room when the teacher paged the office because Tyrone refused to go. Even though Tyrone accompanied Mr. Waller to the office, the principal's threat that he would call Tyrone's parents was all that he was thinking about as they entered the office. One quick move and Tyrone was at the desk, clutching the phone.

Later the behavior consultant accurately identified the punishment → acceleration of aggression/agitation chain that had started with the first warning check and suggested that instead of relying on punishment, the teacher should use a DRO plan for Tyrone. By using a DRO plan with reinforcer exchanges twice a day, the teacher could maintain the same high expectations in her classroom, switching the focus from giving punishment for infractions to giving rewards for following the rules. Along with the DRO plan, the school team set up a clear step-by-step procedure to follow if Tyrone became grossly noncompliant or overtly disruptive in the classroom or school. The steps were as follows:

1. The teacher's direction or request will be repeated to Tyrone and he will be asked to restate it to clarify that he understood.

2. If Tyrone does not follow the teacher's instruction, he will be given a choice to select a more appropriate option (e.g., "You may start working or sit quietly at your desk. It's your choice.").

3. If Tyrone does not select one of the teacher's options and is overtly noncompliant, the teacher will page the office and he will be escorted to a resource area for a time-out to write a "think sheet," a questionnaire to be completed by the student regarding his behavior.

4. If Tyrone refuses to go to the resource area and becomes physically aggressive, the police and parents will be notified and he will be removed from school.

Fortunately, the switch to a DRO plan and the clear directions to the staff and Tyrone about consequences for aggressive behavior resolved the issue. Tyrone earned an average of 84% of his points, and the teacher never had to move past Step 2 because Tyrone always opted to follow directions.

Effective Punishment Options

1. *Losing time with peers is especially effective with older students.* Whether the consequence is losing 1 or 2 minutes of socializing during

passing times or losing the privilege to eat lunch with friends, this consequence can be more effective than many other punishments a teacher routinely gives. The student who could care less about earning an "F" will do anything to avoid missing a moment with friends.

2. *Time-out spent at a desk in the back of a classroom of students who are older is a consequence many students would rather avoid.* Time-out consequences should never be longer than 5 to 10 minutes of quiet, acceptable behavior, and are only effective if they are not an appealing option to the student. To ensure that the time away from class does not become motivating, require the student to complete a "think sheet" before returning to the classroom. Predesigned "think sheets" ask the student to write answers to three or four questions such as the following: "Which classroom rule did you break?" "Why did you break the classroom rule?" "What is the consequence for your breaking the rule?" "What will you do differently next time?"

3. *Require that students who are heard verbally harassing other students or teachers write three complimentary statements about them.* Most students are loathe to put compliments in print, especially if they must think of three new statements each time another instance of verbal harassment occurs. To maintain fairness, write a clear definition of what exactly constitutes verbally harassing behavior.

4. *After clearing the legal aspects of this technique, use audio- or videotape monitoring for a day as a consequence to misbehavior in the classroom.* Select 10 or 20 minutes of the tape and have the student and/or parents take data with you as you watch or listen to the segment. Even if the student is predictably angelic on the day of the taping consequence, be assured that most students will try their hardest to avoid a repetition of this close examination of their behavior in class.

5. *A response cost behavior plan is a point-penalty system with accompanying reinforcement to minimize the disadvantages that accompany punishment.* In a response cost plan, the student starts out with a set number of points, but loses one every time he engages in the unmanageable behavior. Each time the teacher takes away one of the points, the student is technically punished. The student will only have the opportunity to earn a reinforcer at the determined exchange time, if he or she has retained a predetermined number of points. If Barb's unmanageable behaviors are being out of her seat and talking out in class, the teacher can design a response cost plan by assigning 10 points to Barb at the start of each class period. Each time Barb does either of these behaviors during her class she will lose a point. The teacher will assign enough points at the beginning of the interval so that Barb is unlikely to lose all of them. A teacher never wants to go into negative numbers with a response cost plan. Each time that Barb leaves her seat or talks out in class, the teacher will cross off 1 of

the 10 points as she explains to Barb why she has lost the point. To earn a star at the end of the class period, Barb will need to retain a predetermined number of points. For example, Barb might need to retain 6 points at the end of class to earn her star that means that she only lost 4 points. Once or twice a day Barb will have the opportunity to turn in the stars she has earned for a choice of reinforcers.

Using Punishment Effectively:
A Sample Response Cost Plan

Let's look over the shoulders of the Glen Cove School team as they develop a response cost plan for John, a sixth-grade student whose parents recently stopped his Ritalin™ prescription because it did not result in fewer complaints about John's behavior. After the principal and other team members at Glen Cove School had completed Steps 1 through 3 on the Behavior Intervention Planning Form provided in Chapter 2 and were ready to develop some interventions, they decided that one of their strategies would be a response cost plan. They referred to their data to see how often the disruptive behavior was occurring so they could set an interval size and make an estimate about how many points they would give John at the start of each interval. In this plan, John received five points for every interval. The intervals coincided with the end of classes except for the first 10 minutes of school, when he routinely caused disruptions. The team decided that John would have to retain three points at the end of each interval to earn a star. At the two reinforcement exchange times (10:05 a.m. and 2:30 p.m.), he could select a reinforcer if he had earned enough stars. The staff tried to design the plan so that John earned reinforcement 80% of the time. Later, they would make it more difficult for John to earn reinforcement.

Although a response cost plan can result in more rapid behavior change, it should never be used with a student who obsesses about each and every point loss, gradually becoming more agitated. If a student fits this description, then the classroom teacher should opt to use a DRO plan and avoid escalating the aggressive/agitation behavior. A response cost plan should not be used if a criticism trap is operating in the classroom. A teacher who is excessively critical needs a plan that will increase reinforcement. The decision whether to use a DRO or response cost plan often depends on the teacher's personality. Some teachers feel more comfortable giving points, whereas others feel more effective taking them away. If possible, respect the teacher's decision about which type of plan to use.

Although the variations on a basic response cost plan are limitless, first modify this basic plan for one of your unmanageable students before you exercise creativity.

John's Response Cost Plan

Student: John Gage

Teacher: Ms. Adele Towers

School: Glen Cove School

Date: 2/09/99

Problem Behaviors: Use of disrespectful language, noncompliance with teacher's requests and directions, disturbing others with hands, feet, and/or objects

Behavioral Objectives

1. To decrease John's use of disrespectful language with the teacher. Disrespectful language includes rude comments not appropriate in John's classroom: swearing, name calling, and verbal insults.

2. To increase John's compliance with following the teacher's requests and directions. John is compliant when he is following the teacher's instructions and directions. If the teacher asks him to line up with the other children, John will line up. If John is being noisy in line and the teacher reminds him to use a quiet voice, he will begin to use a quiet voice. If John is bopping his pencil on his desk and the teacher asks him to stop, he will put the pencil down within a few moments. Because John's attention frequently wanders, the teacher will not assume that John has heard her directions unless John is looking at her or has indicated that he notices. John will not be penalized for noncompliance when the direction needs to be repeated.

3. To increase John's keeping hands, feet, and objects to himself. John is keeping his hands, feet, and objects to himself when he is not pushing, tripping, touching, poking, butting, or engaging in any similar behavior to another student or person in the school environment.

Punishment Phase

John will start each interval with five points. Whenever he uses disrespectful language with the teacher, is noncompliant with the teacher's instructions and directions, or does not keep hands, feet and objects to himself, the teacher will cross off one point from the five points in the designated time segment. Immediately after the inappropriate behavior occurs (within 5 seconds) the teacher will walk over to John, describe the inappropriate behavior, and cross off the point. John will need three points at the end of the interval to earn his star (see Exhibit 5.1, John's Point Exchange Record).

John will either earn or lose all of the five points during the lunch period. Because individually focused supervision is not possible at those times, John will keep the five points as long as the lunchroom or playground supervisor does not indicate that John has been disruptive. As long as John has followed the supervisor's instructions; kept his hands, feet, and objects to himself; and has used respectful talking with the supervisors, he will keep all five points. If the supervisor reports any infraction of these rules, John will lose all his points during that time.

A brief time-out period will be used if John loses all of his points during an interval. Rather than sitting in the hallway where supervision is minimal and John can chat with other students, John will go to the fifth-grade classroom and complete a think sheet.

Reward Phase

John will begin each interval with five points. If he has retained at least three out of the five points at the end of the interval he will earn a star. There will be two exchange opportunities during each day when John will have the opportunity to exchange his stars for an item or activity from the reinforcer menu. To make the first exchange he will need to have earned all four of the possible stars and to make the second he will need to have earned eight out of the nine possible stars.

The reinforcement menu will contain a choice of several items displayed in written form. Choices may include items such as playing with a Game Boy, reading video tip magazines, playing with the computer, earning a baseball or football card, playing a short game such as dominoes or cards, reading a comic strip book such as *Calvin and Hobbes,* or earning the opportunity to pick a fortune cookie. If John earns his reinforcement exchanges on Friday, there will be coupons that he can take home that will enable him to get a special video, a homework pass, or McDonald's for supper.

This behavior program will only succeed if John desires the items on the reinforcer menu. Some days the teacher might want to add an additional option. If something is never selected, replace it with another item. Sometimes the silliest ideas become the best reinforcers.

In addition to the reinforcement at exchange time, John will keep an ongoing record of his daily point total in a bankbook. Another reinforcer list will be developed for this grand point total. Maintaining a grand point total will serve to motivate John when he has lost too many points by 10:00 a.m. for an exchange that day. The teacher can remind John that the points he earns still count for the big item. John's reinforcement menu for the grand point total will include special highly motivating rewards such as earning back the privilege of walking in the hall between classes without a monitor or earning a trip with his parents to a skating rink.

Time	Points	Star
8:00 - 8:10	1 1 1 1 1	
8:10 - 8:45	1 1 1 1 1	
8:45 - 9:10	1 1 1 1 1	
9:10 - 10:00	1 1 1 1 1	
10:05 - 10:15	a.m. exchange time: 4/4 stars needed for an exchange	
10:15 - 10:45	1 1 1 1 1	
10:45 - 11:05	1 1 1 1 1	
11:05 - 11:55	1 1 1 1 1	
11:55 - 12:20	1 1 1 1 1	
12:20 - 12:40	1 1 1 1 1	
12:40 - 1:15	1 1 1 1 1	
1:15 - 1:35	1 1 1 1 1	
1:35 - 2:00	1 1 1 1 1	
2:00 - 2:30	1 1 1 1 1	
2:30	p.m. exchange time: 8/9 stars needed for an exchange	

McEwan, E., & Damer, M. *Managing Unmanageable Students: Practical Solutions for Administrators.*
© 2000, Corwin Press, Inc.

EXHIBIT 5.1 John's Point Exchange Record

The teacher will praise John for appropriate behaviors (e.g., in seat, following teacher's instructions, independent working, showing self-control, respecting property) and academic behaviors (e.g., task-oriented, completion of task, correct answer, imaginative answer).

Staff Coordination Roles

1. Ms. Towers, John's teacher, will design daily point sheets and will adapt the end-of-the-week data sheet.

2. Ms. Towers will develop a written room chart with the three behavioral rules listed.

3. Ms. Towers will design the reinforcement menus (a.m. and p.m. exchanges and the long-term one). The school principal will assist by purchasing motivating items that are not currently available (e.g., a Walkman).

4. Before implementation, the school social worker will explain the behavior system to John and his parents.

5. This program will begin on February 16.

Implementation Guidelines

- Reinforce, reinforce, reinforce. A student who does not typically think about the effects of his or her actions requires positive behavioral feedback in the process of developing appropriate behaviors. Praise should be behavior descriptive. Reinforce at least every 5 minutes. Because response cost is a punishment strategy, frequent positive feedback for good behavior is essential.

- Be consistent in removing points for inappropriate behavior. Do not give warnings or threats about points lost. John either loses points or keeps them.

- Make the point removal specific. John is not being punished in a personal sense, rather his behavior is being consequated. Stay calm, be brief, maintain a neutral face and a matter-of-fact voice tone. Never grind in a point loss.

Issues for the Team to Explore
in Team Meetings

1. Is John's success rate at least 80%? If not, what adjustments can be made?

2. Do definitions of the target behaviors such as following teacher's directions and instructions need more specification for consistency?

3. How will the plan change? When will John need more points for a star? Is John ready for four points in an interval? These changes should be the next two steps.

4. Are the reinforcers motivating for John? Is a surprise reinforcer sometimes added to the menu?

John is on his way to classroom success. What about *your* unmanageable students? Although developing and implementing a behavioral intervention plan is an important aspect of managing the behavior of an unmanageable student, it is not the only consideration. Chapters 6 and 7 discuss the other pieces of the behavior management puzzle—effective teaching and academic success. The best intervention plans will fail miserably if instruction is ineffective and students are not achieving academic success.

CHAPTER SIX

Effective Teachers Equal Effective Students

Critical Teaching Behaviors

Take a mental stroll down the hallways of your school with a clipboard in hand. Imagine that it contains a complete list of your staff members. After the names there are two columns headed "effective teacher" and "ineffective teacher." As you pause at each doorway, mark the column that best describes the teacher you see. Once you have completed this imaginary exercise in teacher evaluation, spend a few moments to consider what happens when a student is placed into the classroom of one of those ineffective teachers. You already know the answer: The odds of that student's academic success will decline precipitously. We call it the "Bermuda Triangle" because just as ships and planes seem to disappear into the mythical Bermuda Triangle, students disappear academically and behaviorally into the educational one.

The model students in your school will no doubt endure the year somewhat stoically, learning far less than they might have in the classroom of an effective teacher but patiently daydreaming through the endless hours (nearly 1,000 of them in an elementary classroom). But the "Calvins" of your school who resemble their unmanageable comic strip namesake are far more likely to act out than tune out. The student with behavior problems has not developed the daydreaming skills that help our model student cope with the confusion or tedium that is pervasive in the ineffective teacher's classroom. Unmanageable students often come from chaotic home environments, have learning problems, or experience high levels of impulsivity and distractibility. These students are more likely to respond to ineffective teaching by snapping off rubber bands, distracting other students, or "smarting off" to the teacher.

You can no doubt relate to the frustration of these students if you recall your worst graduate course or administrative inservice. If your tune-out skills were not so finely honed, you might have been tempted to make a little trouble yourself.

Behavior specialists know that the heart of good classroom management is effective instruction. If Carla, who spent most of fourth grade in your office poses no problem this year, chances are that the fifth grade teacher should get the credit. If you observe Carla this year, you are likely to see her teacher employing teaching methods that reflect the most valid research practices. Carla is responding to effective instruction.

Critical Teaching Behaviors

There are many critical teaching behaviors that impact student behavior. We will consider five of the most important, namely, how a teacher does the following:

1. Plans the physical environment.
2. Establishes structure and routine to build a comfortable level of predictability.
3. Monitors student behavior when not directly teaching.
4. Teaches organizational skills, the nature of learning tasks, and the strategies needed to complete the learning task.
5. Uses an animated teaching style to convey enthusiasm for learning.

Planning the Physical Environment

The effective teacher plans the physical environment to minimize disruptive behaviors. Solving an unmanageable student problem is sometimes as easy as helping a teacher rearrange his or her classroom! As principals, we were always secretly delighted when our room arrangement suggestions to a teacher resolved a student discipline problem within 24 hours. All of our problems should be solved so easily! Because this very basic solution will sometimes produce a dramatic reduction in a student's disruptive behaviors, we recommend starting with a survey of the physical classroom. For the more than five decades that we have collectively worked in schools, we have watched the educational pendulum swing several times between one best practice recommending that students sit at individual desks in rows to another best practice recommending that students sit clustered around tables or in pods of desks. What has never changed, however, is what well-designed research studies tell us about the relationship of seating arrangements and student behavior. Whether these studies are investigating disadvantaged or high-performing students, the results clearly show that an increase in physical space between students leads to increased on-task time and decreased disruptive behavior. In classrooms where students have more space between each other, teachers are even rated by their students as more sensitive and friendly (Paine et al., 1983). Because fewer behavior disruptions occur in classrooms where students are spaced with more distance between each other, the teacher has fewer behavior problems to correct and can focus more energy on teaching and giving students positive feedback.

Because of the current emphasis on cooperative learning groups, many teachers find it preferable to have students permanently grouped around a table or with their desks pushed into small "pods." Teachers would rather not have the students move their individually spaced desks together every time a group learning activity is scheduled. You can help these teachers understand that group seating arrangements often lead to increased behavior problems and that teaching their students to move their desks together quickly and quietly for group activities would be time well spent. During the rest of the day, individual student desks can be spaced apart from each other, especially when students are working on independent seatwork. Although a highly motivated, high-performing, nondistractible student will continue to excel in spite of sitting in a pod, most students do not fall into that category.

In the workplace, desks are arranged into cubicles behind dividers for sound reasons. Any boss knows that employees will work more diligently when distractions are reduced. How many adults do their best work when seated in a group with some of their closest friends? The temptation to socialize is too strong for most adults, just as it is for students. A contemporary technology magazine described the ensuing chaos that erupted when advertising agencies experimented with unconventional workstations during the 1990s. The experiments were cut short by the employees' need for personal workspace and "the cubicle survived" (Berger, 1999, p. 81).

Because every classroom has one or two students whose high level of distractibility triggers unmanageable behaviors during independent work times, we suggest that classrooms have one or two desks located in the quietest, most nondistracting location. A desk facing the wall between two filing cabinets or tucked in between the "L" shape formed by the juncture of a bookcase and a wall can serve as an "I do my best work here" office area. These student "offices" should not be viewed as punishment areas, but rather as strategic places where a student can work undistracted. Before journal writing time, the teacher can say to the student who has a difficult time concentrating during writing and often disturbs other children, "Take your journal to your office area where you do your best work." Eventually, the teacher will want distractible students to recognize that they do their best work in a quiet area away from distractions and move there without prompting. When an easily distractible student independently chooses the office space without a reminder cue, the teacher has taught an important lifetime strategy for completing work.

In classrooms with younger students, pay close attention to those times of the day when the teacher asks students to sit on a rug for story time, discussion of the calendar, or "show and tell." Many elementary classrooms are not physically large enough to allow for an ample rug area, and as a result the younger, wigglier children are crammed into an elbow-jostling space. Within minutes after moving to the cramped areas, the students' on-task rate plummets with the teacher's corrections of students' misbehavior concurrently increasing. For the student with unmanageable behaviors, the unpredictable environment can quickly trigger disruptive behavior. We explain to teachers in this situation that although they want the nurturing ambiance resulting from the more informal "flop down on the rug" atmosphere, the environment is working against what they hope to achieve and more conventional seating is much to be preferred.

If the rug area is large enough to space the children apart adequately, the teacher of younger children will typically have at least one very active child who cannot handle the loss of boundaries that an open rug presents. This wiggly child, who will invariably scoot over to invade another child's space or flop around on the rug like a beached dolphin, needs a separate carpet square or a small chair to sit in during the rug times. The chair or carpet square should not be viewed as a punishment, but rather as a strategic place that helps a child keep his or her body under control in order to listen to the story or participate in the discussion. The teacher can explain to the child, "You do your best sitting in group when you sit on the chair."

The placement of the teacher's desk also affects student behavior. Whether students are in kindergarten or in high school, they will be on-task more consistently and will display fewer disruptive behaviors when they know they are closely monitored. The student who looks engaged in work when viewed from behind can be mouthing quiet insulting comments to another child or drawing gang symbols on a paper shielded from the teacher's view. Unless the teacher's desk is used only after school hours, it should be located in clear view of all of the students. Many students will decide whether to follow the classroom rules or engage in disruptive behavior depending on whether the teacher is watching. This teacher dynamic relates so highly to increased student on-task behavior that researchers have coined the term *with-itness*, referring to the teacher's perceived ability to have eyes in the back of the head (O'Shea, O'Shea, & Rosenberg, 1998). Teachers who pause at their desks momentarily to get materials needed for the lesson or to read the lunch menu present the "illusion" of awareness more effectively when their desks are in front of the classroom and in clear view. Their unobstructed views of students' faces enable them to monitor student activity more closely and nip disruptive behaviors at the onset.

In most cases, the student with unmanageable behavior should be seated closest to the spot where the teacher most commonly stands. Proximity enables the teacher to instruct and monitor the classroom, subtly providing redirection cues when needed. When the teacher instructs students to take out their maps of Australia, he or she can use a touch cue on the shoulder or a gentle pat on the desk to remind the targeted student to open the desktop and find the map. When the teacher explains tomorrow's assignment, the moment the student with unmanageable behaviors starts to extend his body into space with the intention of bothering a nearby student, the teacher can give a hand cue, refocusing the student to the ongoing instructions. For a more comprehensive list of classroom environmental modifications, see *The Principal's Guide to Attention Deficit Hyperactivity Disorder* (McEwan, 1998a).

Using Structure and Routine to Establish Predictability

The effective teacher uses structure and routine to establish a comfortable level of predictability.

> Forewarning is the process of giving a visual picture of the future. Slow-to-adapt kids need to know what the future holds. . . . Some kids need to be told hours, days, even weeks in advance what they will be doing. This gives them time to ask their questions, and mentally prepare. (Kurcinka, 1991, p. 141)

Adults as well as children want and need a certain level of predictability to accomplish their most productive work. Students who are distractible or come from chaotic home environments require an even higher level of structure to ensure the predictability needed to make their world a more manageable place. When teachers raise concerns that structure and creativity are incompatible, assure them that they can and do coexist by describing the end product of a spellbinding orchestra concert or a dance company's recital, clearly two examples of the marriage of structure and creativity. Staff members who create structured classrooms will typically have fewer students with discipline problems because they have learned how to make the classroom environment work for them to prevent those problems.

The following are five primary ways to establish predictability:

1. Post visible classroom rules.

2. Post schedules and develop a structured sequence of activities.

3. Articulate behavioral expectations frequently.

4. Provide advance organizers while teaching lessons.

5. Set frequent, short-term goals.

Classroom Rules

Posting classroom rules serves to remind both the teacher and the students of behavioral expectations. Before the school year begins, a teacher should develop between four and six clearly worded classroom rules, posting them in highly visible locations in the classroom. The rules should be stated positively and convey exactly what the students are expected to do. Examples of clear and positive classroom rules include the following:

Keep hands and feet to self.

Raise your hand when you want to speak.

Wait for your turn during group activities and use a quiet voice.

Whenever a student violates one of the rules, the organized classroom teacher refers to the posted chart before following through with the consequence that always occurs when that rule is broken. The teacher may choose to give a verbal reminder as a consequence when a child does not follow the rule to raise a hand while waiting to be called on during discussion. If a student does not remember to keep hands, feet, and objects to self, the consequence might be answering a set of questions related to the rule infraction. The teacher who has posted explicit rules and has decided on specific consequences when a student breaks one of the rules is more likely to have students follow those rules consistently. In contrast, a disorganized teacher treats each rule-breaking incident as a novel situation, and students in that type of classroom never know what their teacher will do next. They may ask themselves, "Why not break a rule when the teacher ignores the infraction some of the time?" All students are more apt to think before engaging in misbehavior when clearly posted rules are visible and when they know that the teacher expects them to follow those rules.

Organized teachers will teach the rules during the first week or two of school, demonstrating to students what following the rules "looks like." Some teachers will play an amusing game where they display a behavior and ask the students to mark whether they were following the rules or not. Once organized teachers know that every student understands the expectations for the classroom, during the remainder of the year they will periodically praise students who are following the rules in order to provide additional motivation: "Everyone in row one remembered to raise hands. Row one may line up first for lunch."

Daily Schedules

The effective teacher posts a daily schedule that is large enough to be seen by every student. Throughout the day, the teacher can refer to the schedule, drawing the student's attention to the next schedule change and the rules associated with it. The younger the children in the class, the more the teacher will need to use this organizational strategy. A structured early-childhood teacher will often display Velcro-backed squares with pictures depicting each activity change. Every time the class moves from the morning group area to the play area or to the book corner, one child will move the card describing the next activity into a highlighted spot as the teacher talks about the upcoming change. As students advance to higher grade levels, the need for advance warning about minor schedule changes reduces somewhat, but middle or high school teachers will still find that more disorganized or volatile students display fewer disruptive behaviors when transitions are clearly defined.

Behavioral Expectations

The effective teacher takes the time to articulate behavioral expectations frequently, particularly when they are changing. Every time a class activity changes, the teacher's demeanor changes, the rules tend to change, the materials required for the task change, and sometimes even the visual field in front of the student changes. The screaming that is acceptable and even helpful for winning an exciting dodgeball game in gym class has to be stopped when the math teacher, Mr. Macklin, directs students to walk quietly down the hallway back to the classroom. As soon as the students reach his classroom, Mr. Macklin expects them to walk directly to their desks and locate all of the materials needed for math class. He knows that a smooth transition between activities should only take between 30 seconds to a minute. Because his students have three different subject area teachers during the day, they are responsible for remembering the subtle rules that surround instruction in each room. A student who is strategic, highly motivated, and organized will automatically carry out the required tasks and remember the rules. The other students, especially those with unmanageable behaviors, will need short reminders when the environmental demands change.

If Mr. Macklin reminds his students before they leave the gym to stay quietly in line, keep hands to self, and take out the math materials when they enter the classroom, they are more likely to transition smoothly to the classroom. By stating the behavioral expectations for the next activity, he is ensuring that more students will follow them. Anticipating the difficulty that some students might have in transitioning from a boisterous gym class to his more subdued math class, Mr. Macklin may play quiet classical music as the students begin working the challenge problem he has written on the board.

We recommend that you invite disorganized teachers to spend time in a classroom like Mr. Macklin's, observing and taking notes on how time is used, how transitions are structured, and how students are frequently alerted to behavioral expectations. If a less-organized teacher can observe someone like Mr. Macklin in action and then participate in a follow-up conference regarding the techniques, there may well be fewer unmanageable students referred from the teacher's classroom.

Many teachers use signals when students' behavior during transition times becomes too boisterous. Whether they choose to flick the lights, put their hand in the air, count to three or ask everyone to put their finger on their mouth, these teachers have devised a concrete indicator to signal that everyone is expected to pause, quiet down, and then get on with the task at hand. When the signal is pervasive and highly visible, even the child with unmanageable behaviors who is not focused on the teacher's discernible irritation with the commotion will be more likely to begin following his or her directions.

Advance Organizers

Effective teachers give students ample opportunities to get ready to learn. These teachers' lessons begin with advance organizers, telling the students how the lessons will proceed. To create additional structure, the teacher might write one or two words on the board about each subactivity in the lesson; for example,

> First we will work in groups and complete the worksheets, then we will return to our desks and work on our geoboards, and finally we'll finish the math facts sheet. If everyone works hard, we should have time to put the number of math facts we answered correctly on our rocket charts.

Students with unmanageable behaviors are more likely to act out during a part of a lesson that is difficult and tedious because they are unable to think strategically about how quickly a part of the lesson will be finished. They get lost in the moment, consumed by how much they want to do anything else but the activity that is in front of them. If the teacher has focused these students on the sequence of activities, they are more likely to persevere through a difficult part, realizing that it will soon be over.

In the aforementioned math class, Reesa, a somewhat volatile student, is less likely to throw the math facts sheet that she finds so difficult into the garbage when she remembers that yesterday she answered two more problems than the day before. If she can sit quietly for the 5-minute fact sheet, she will be able to record her score on the rocket chart in a few minutes. She glances up at the board where the teacher has written the math agenda and continues working. The teacher's structure helped her make a good choice.

Short-Term Goals

Effective teachers also set frequent short-term goals for each subactivity within a lesson or day, providing more opportunities for positive feedback and helping to focus students who are unable to set goals for themselves. For example, at the appropriate part in the math lesson, the teacher might say, "Each group should try to solve all four geoboard problems. See if you can get four correct answers." Later, when the teacher provides feedback on the answers, he or she can compliment each group that met the goal. Because students with unmanageable behaviors usually do not think strategically about what they want to accomplish before working on a task, the teacher's specific reminders, if realistic, can focus them to the demands of the task. Although habitually using such structure for all lessons can seem repetitive and tiresome, this approach will increase predictability and gradually develop strategy awareness for the student with unmanageable behaviors as well as for many other students.

Active Monitoring

The effective teacher is actively monitoring the classroom when not directly teaching. Although active monitoring exponentially increases a teacher's *with-itness* factor, it is surprising how many teachers do not take full advantage of this simple technique to reduce disruptive student behavior (Gunter, Shores, & Rasmussen, 1995). Whether students are working independently on seatwork or in small groups, the teacher who moves around to every corner of the room provides a consistent reminder that helps students stay focused on their work. When teachers are not directly teaching, they should be monitoring if they intend to minimize disruptive behaviors. Teachers who are effectively monitoring avoid lingering too long in one spot while still assuring that their paths frequently pass by the desk or group where the student with unmanageable behaviors is working. By using their eyes to scan other sections of the classroom while walking around the room, teachers attain an even greater sense of with-itness.

Teachers who are actively monitoring ask questions, give students academic and behavioral feedback, and check to see if the students are solving problems correctly. Teachers who monitor with the demeanor of police personnel have to be encouraged to provide brief assistance and positive feedback in addition to intervening when they see off-task behaviors. Monitoring with the sole intention of catching behavioral infractions will not only increase the teacher's stress level, but can readily send the student with unmanageable behavior into an explosive mode.

Because monitoring is just as important for preventing unmanageable behavior out on the playground, in the hallways, during assemblies, or in the lunchroom, employ management by walking around to ensure that your staff is consistently monitoring in those settings where they are in charge. Do the lunchroom supervisors stand chatting to the side until a disruption demands their attention, or are they walking up and down the rows of students, briefly chatting, commenting, and redirecting? Are the teaching assistants who monitor the playground strategically located around the physical area, using eyes and walking patterns to create the illusion of being everywhere? Unless you routinely walk the building, ensuring that staff members are monitoring at a high level, chances are that some of them will fall into poor habits. If you model effective monitoring to your school employees, commenting on the alert behavior you notice them using, pointing out a lunchroom group that could use an adult standing nearby within a three-foot radius, or simply engaging them in brief pleasant conversation that does not distract from their task at hand, you will raise the monitoring quotient of your entire school.

Organizational Skills

The effective teacher teaches organizational skills, the nature of learning tasks, and the strategies needed to complete the tasks. Many students with unmanageable behaviors are consistently disorganized. They are more likely to arrive at class without the required pens and textbooks, to forget to take their homework home, to forget to complete the homework when they do take it home, and to claim they have studied for a test after 5 minutes of superficial review. We shake our heads at such forgetfulness, tending to view their lack of responsibility as willful negligence. Too often, however, the disorganized student has not learned the school survival skills needed to function in the classroom. Homework completion, time management, asking questions for clarification, and studying for tests are skills that the disorganized student is lacking. Unfortunately, this disorganization can easily lead to off-task behaviors or start a chain of punishment consequences that can quickly escalate. Brad's attitude about his missing homework triggers his first warning check on the board. During the opening review of the homework, Brad's resulting inattention leads to a second warning check. By the time the class has started working on new material, Brad is drawing skulls on his folder and has tuned out the teacher.

When the middle school principal observed Brad in the classroom, she realized how difficult it was to separate his inappropriate behaviors from his pervasive forgetfulness. Her observation revealed that the teacher's natural consequences for Brad's disorganization provided the main trigger for his unmanageable behaviors. When the principal investigated the two classes in which Brad did not have problems, she observed that those teachers did not automatically assume that their students had the organizational skills needed for success in the course. These teachers required their students to set up notebooks at the beginning of the year, they wrote homework assignments on the board each day pausing a few moments as students copied them into their notebooks, and they always talked about the learning strategies required for new tasks. They reviewed students' notebooks at regular intervals and recognized that because every classroom has many disorganized students, teacher attention to these details helped everyone in the class. These teachers did not lower expectations, but neither did they assume that all students had the necessary school survival skills. They habitually incorporated the following strategies into all of their teaching activities.

1. *Teachers who encourage a high degree of organization do not automatically assume that their students are actively thinking about the answers to questions.* To encourage a higher rate of active thinking, these teachers frequently require everyone to write down the answer to a question. These teachers actively monitor and stand by students who are not writing to help them learn to follow the instructions.

2. *Teachers who encourage a high degree of organization spend only a small portion of each class period reviewing homework from the day before.* Once these teachers know what material needs to be retaught and what material the majority of students have completed accurately, they move on with their lesson. If students correct homework in class, the answers are posted on an overhead to minimize the time involved in the process.

3. *Teachers who encourage a high degree of organization provide organized study sheets for students before tests, quizzes, or projects.* They provide a clear and detailed syllabus for older students.

4. *Teachers who encourage a high degree of organization assign homework or projects that can be completed by students independently at home.* They know that if projects require parents to build or construct portions of the assignment, students whose parents are uninvolved will be penalized.

5. *Teachers who encourage a high degree of organization return homework or projects promptly to provide feedback and affirm that all assignments are meaningful.* These teachers know that if students do not receive graded homework or receive it weeks later, they will be more likely to assume that its completion is unimportant.

6. *Teachers who encourage a high degree of organization talk about specific parts of assignments that are necessary for successful completion.* These teachers may also talk about strategies they would use if completing the assignment. For example, if the students are assigned two paragraphs about the Civil War, organized teachers will remind students when

the assignment is given that grammar and spelling need to be accurate. They will encourage students to put a check mark next to their name after they reread the paper out loud during their final editing.

7. *Teachers who encourage a high degree of organization always talk about what will be learned, why it will be learned, how it will be learned, and what specific strategies the student should use to learn the material.*

8. *Teachers who encourage a high degree of organization in an early childhood or primary classroom will ask questions when students do not follow directions in order to encourage them to focus on what they should think about to complete the task.* The following scenario describes a teacher who understands that teaching organizational skills often accompanies teaching subject material:

Ms. Reddy: Students, I want you to close your math book, get out a pencil, and put your name on top of the volcano assignment I'm passing out. How many people can follow those directions? (Ms. Reddy passes out papers as most of the students follow her directions. She notices that although Cornell and Jamie put their math books away, they are now staring into space.)

Ms. Reddy: Bryan, what should Cornell and Jamie be doing now?

Bryan: Getting pencils and writing their names.

If Cornell and Jamie follow through on the directions, Ms. Reddy continues with the next step of the lesson. If they do not, she prompts them to write their names at the top of the page, knowing that in another month or two they will begin to recognize that this procedure is always followed in her classroom. Whereas other students learned more quickly to follow through on three- and four-step directions, Cornell and Jamie still focus on the first step and forget to move on to the next one. Ms. Reddy wants to establish good habits from the beginning of the school year, but she knows that she will have to teach those habits to some of the students. When she was an inexperienced teacher, she expected all of her students to "know" how to follow instructions, but she soon realized that scolding students when they did not follow directions was not nearly as effective as teaching them organizational skills from the beginning.

9. *Teachers who encourage a high degree of organization in upper-grade, middle, or high school classrooms recognize that note taking will keep students more actively involved in learning.* They also know that note taking is a skill that students will only acquire gradually after much practice. These teachers expect students to have notebooks or blank concept maps on their desks during discussions or lectures, and they highlight points

during the period when all students should be writing. These teachers actively monitor to ensure that everyone takes notes.

Teachers who encourage a high degree of organization by consistently teaching the above organizational skills will be more likely to meet the needs of students whose lack of school survival skills lead to unmanageable behaviors. Marya, a student whose noncompliant and rude behavior was most frequently triggered by her inability to complete homework assignments or follow directions, is one such student. When the school team met to formulate a plan, they decided that Marya needed to develop more effective and consistent organizational strategies. Mr. Lukas, the principal, suggested to Marya's teacher that a daily assignment sheet or book would help her develop strategies for completing homework, studying for tests, and noting important announcements. Because he recognized that initially Marya would need assistance in writing down notes, announcements, and assignments on a consistent basis, he reminded the teacher that she would need to scan the class quickly and direct Marya to pull out the book until this procedure became a habit. In the beginning, the teacher would need to note if Marya was not writing down something important and remind her that "this goes in the book." Eventually, the team members wanted Marya to become self-reliant in her use of the assignment book as an organizational strategy. Marya's parents were asked to check the notebook every night and talk to her about her assignments, which they remembered to do most of the time. Because Mr. Lukas periodically asked the teacher how Marya's notebook was working out, the teacher was motivated and remembered to consistently use this adaptation. With the combination of parental support, the teacher's organization, and the principal's monitoring, Marya's rate of homework completion rose dramatically. With decreased frustration, her unmanageable behaviors were no longer an issue.

Animated Teaching Styles

The effective teacher has an animated teaching style that conveys enthusiasm for learning. If you attend a corporate training seminar, whether the topic is grant writing or using cooperative communication skills on a new team project, you will notice the theatrical teaching style of the presenter. To capture the audience's attention, the presenter actively moves around the room, uses clearly outlined overheads, asks motivating questions, tells the audience how the new learning will impact their lives, and provides opportunities for the audience to practice the new skills. Just as the corporate teacher employs theatrical skills as a part of effective teaching, the enthusiastic delivery of many modern educational consultants provides relief for those of us who remember the ineffectual presentations we sat through 20 years ago during what seemed to be endless school district inservice days. Humor, exaggerated affect, and direct eye contact with the audience enhance the presentation of any educational consultant who hopes to be invited back for a repeat performance.

Whether a teacher is lecturing, conducting small group work activities, or facilitating a learning game activity, his or her theatrical style will directly contribute to the students' cooperation, attitude, and participation in the learning session. Teachers who want to maximize the odds of keeping the student with unmanageable behaviors on-task need to use a variety of theatrical strategies to maintain a high interest level. To enhance their theatrical art of teaching, elementary teachers use exaggerated affect and overenthusiastic voice tones to emphasize the wonder of the new concepts they are teaching. Relating to their students in a "cooler" framework, middle and high school teachers must tone down that exaggerated approach and rely more on subtle humor and silly puns to punctuate their lessons. Whatever the age level of the students they are teaching, however, engaging teachers convey their enthusiasm regarding the subject matter through their energetic movement around the classroom, dramatic pauses after vivid examples, use of gestures to punctuate concepts, and variance in their voice and tempo.

Your Role as an Instructional Leader

Your role as an instructional leader is to supervise, evaluate, affirm, and encourage the five teaching behaviors we have discussed in this chapter. You will receive a double bonus as you highlight the importance of effective teaching in your school: Student achievement will rise in direct proportion to the structure and organizational focus of your classrooms and the incidents of unmanageable student behavior will decline.

CHAPTER SEVEN

Learning

The Magic Wand for Good Behavior

How would you feel if you suddenly found yourself sitting in a semester-long graduate-level particle physics class for 2 hours each day? Would copying answers during cooperative group activities alleviate your rising anxiety as you sat amidst individuals who were talking about concepts for which you had no underlying knowledge? At what point would you stop listening to the meaningless discussion and begin to think about something more relevant? Would you start to feel antsy at some point and find yourself wishing you could run laps around the building rather than sit in that classroom for one more minute? Your escalating feelings of anxiety would no doubt be similar to those shared by many of our schools' unmanageable students who lack the basic skills needed for their schoolwork. Hopeless frustration can trigger unmanageable behaviors that may thwart your staff's best attempts to resolve them. Students in these situations become motivated to escape their classrooms. Sitting in the hall, writing sentences in the office, or going to a detention room are all preferable alternatives for students who want out of the classroom, away from work for which they do not have the necessary skills.

Experienced teachers have long recognized a relationship between student achievement and behavior. They will not be surprised that researchers at the Educational Testing Service reported that students with discipline problems have lower test scores (Portner, 1998). After analyzing the discipline records and achievement test scores of 16,000 students surveyed between 1988 and 1994, researchers found that students who had committed minor or more serious offenses scored 10% lower on achievement tests in mathematics, reading, social science, and science than students who did not have such discipline problems (Portner, 1998). Does problem behavior result in poor achievement or, does poor achievement, or more important, the inability to achieve success academically, cause many problem behaviors?

The answer to this basic question is complex. Do students misbehave because they are not learning or do students do poorly in school because they are more adept at making trouble than making good grades? Our experience suggests that with few exceptions, children begin school with an eagerness and desire to learn. Only when the system breaks down in meeting their needs (e.g., ineffective teaching, overloaded classrooms, poorly defined objectives and curriculum, or problems such as learning difficulties or Attention Deficit Hyperactivity Disorder [ADHD]) do students turn to making mischief as a cover-up for their academic failure. They are highly skilled at diverting educators' attention from the real problem: lack of success at learning. In reality, most students would prefer to be thought of as a "smart aleck" or a troublemaker than to be labeled "disabled," "slow," or "at-risk."

A disturbing relationship exists between low reading achievement and the delinquency rate of our country's young people.

> Low reading levels tend to predict the likelihood of the onset of serious delinquency. Longitudinally, poor reading achievement and delinquency appear to mutually influence each other. Prior reading level predicted later subsequent delinquency . . . [moreover] poor reading achievement increased the chances of serious delinquency persisting over time. (Huizinga, Loeber, & Thornberry, 1991, p. 17)

One of the most powerful ways to improve the behavior of unmanageable students is to find curriculum and teaching methods to ensure their academic success, especially in learning to read, write, and do mathematics. With these abilities firmly in hand, students who might be tempted to act out to gain recognition, attention, and self-esteem will find their needs for affirmation met through genuine achievement in school.

How can teachers keep all students in their classrooms interested, involved, and pressing forward academically? The challenges are all too familiar to the average teacher. If the work is too difficult, the students are confused and grow frustrated. If the learning tasks are too easy, the students get bored and tune out. In either case, the potential for behavior problems looms just over the horizon. We call these dynamics the 80% Commandment and the 100% Snore.

Confused or Bored: The Two-Edged Sword

The 80% Commandment

The relationship between students' accuracy with schoolwork and their subsequent behavior is described by the 80% Commandment: "Thou shall not expect a student to do a learning task when he or she does not have the skills to complete the task with 80% success. Otherwise, that student will either act out or tune out." Today's frustrated students who lack basic skills most often respond by acting out.

If you want to check out the 80% Commandment for yourself, observe two or three first graders read a selection in which their accuracy is less than 80%. Watch their movements as they struggle to say the next word, sometimes guessing, sometimes trying in vain to decode. Within 5 minutes of working at this high frustration level, the most tranquil child will begin to squirm, shifting from side to side, rubbing his or her eyes, and looking away from the book. Many first graders put into this situation will look like perfect candidates for Ritalin™ as their hyperactivity and inattention escalate off the charts.

One of the authors wrote the following after spending 2 days observing Kimberly, a struggling second grader described by her teacher as noncompliant and persistently off-task:

> Even though Kimberly could read predictable stories with related pictures, the first time she tried to read the words in the text without the pictures she correctly decoded only 30% of them. When I observed her reading the story again, she appeared to have committed more words to memory, but her accuracy was only 40%. As Kimberly encountered words she did not know, I observed that her squirming increased and her attention decreased. She was trying to please the teacher but was unable to do the work successfully. She may have memorized the sequential text of the stories, but the individual words were not in her long-term memory. No behavior management program or motivational system will be effective until she is reading text with which she has at least 80% to 90% success from the first reading.

Resolving Kimberly's discipline problem required changing the curriculum to a carefully sequenced phonics program. Once Kimberly had mastered the individual sound-spelling correspondences and could independently decode all of the text she encountered, her noncompliance in reading class was no longer an issue.

The 100% Snore

The flip side of the 80% Commandment is a less frequent trigger for disruptive behavior that we call the 100% Snore. Students who have mastered the daily work in their classroom and who do not experience the challenge of learning new material will tune out or act out in much the same way as the frustrated student does. If a third-grade student who can do sixth-grade math makes rude comments to the teacher as the class works on third grade-level multiplication facts, investigate whether a lack of challenge is triggering the unmanageable behavior. If a first-grade reader who is reading fourth and fifth grade-level books at home becomes disruptive during the choral reading of a beginning reading book, investigate whether the lack of challenge is triggering the unmanageable behavior. Just as undue frustration with instruction can trigger problem behaviors, so too can class activities and assignments that the student can easily complete with 100% accuracy.

Solutions to the Two-Edged Sword

How can a principal eliminate these triggers to disruptive behavior that occur when instruction is too difficult or too easy for a given child? The following are three readily available solutions:

1. Retool your grouping strategies to better meet the needs of all students.
2. Fine-tune instructional strategies to increase on-task behavior.
3. Take a closer look at the sequence of instruction to make sure that all of the components of effective instruction are systematically included.

Retool Your Grouping Strategies

Do you struggle with the issue of grouping in your school? You are not alone. Whatever you are doing, there is always an expert or a research study to tell you that you are doing it wrong. Or, maybe you are not and just think you are! Before you despair, do your homework and differentiate effective grouping practices from grouping myths. Even though many of the books and journal articles written during the 1990s claim that mixed ability groups are always more effective, an exhaustive review of the literature on types of groups and student achievement reveals no valid research studies supporting that position. During our investigation of this subject, we were surprised to find that not one large-scale, well-designed experiment has ever been conducted that follows students over several years to evaluate the impact of skill grouping (i.e., homogeneous grouping). Most of the research on grouping issues is more than 30 years old and was conducted before current special education services were in place. Even though grouping has been one of the most hotly debated issues in education during the past 50 years, valid data does not exist to support either mixed ability grouping or same skill grouping approach as being more effective.

Grouping Patterns: Heterogeneous Groups

In schools throughout the country, teachers group their students into one or a combination of six different grouping patterns. Which grouping patterns are used most widely in your school and for what reasons?

Cooperative groups. In cooperative groups, five to seven students of varying abilities are placed together to complete a specific short-term project or task. In some classrooms, cooperative groups remain together as a unit for an extended period of time, with the majority of assignments and projects being completed in a cooperative way. In other instances, cooperative groups change every few days.

Whole-group instruction. A second variation within the heterogeneous grouping category occurs when students of diverse ability levels but at the same grade level and in the same classroom are taught as a whole by their teacher. Instruction is delivered to the whole group on a somewhat regular basis and there are few, if any, attempts to modify instruction to meet the needs of diverse learners.

Multi-age classrooms. The third variation of the heterogeneous grouping pattern is a modern resurrection of the K-8 one-room schoolhouse (several grades in one room), with a new wrinkle, the developmentally appropriate approach. This approach is less an instructional methodology than a philosophical belief—that children will mature and grow into their skills if the pressures of specific grade-level expectations are removed. The quality of "academic press" that might be seen in a more traditional grade-level classroom is frequently supplanted by a more relaxed developmental approach.

Grouping Patterns: Homogeneous Groups

Tracking within a grade level. This type of grouping refers to the much-despised rigid intellectual ability groups that many adults still remember from their childhood. Perhaps only the students in the Buzzard and the Turkey groups disliked their groups, whereas the Eagles soared! The students at a specific grade are divided into high, medium, and low groups based on intelligence quotient measures, past performance, and/or achievement test scores. Once the groups are sorted, students typically stay in their original group classification "forever."

For example, there might be a high, medium, and low class at each grade level, each with a different teacher. The curriculum and instructional methods are only slightly adapted for the stratified groups, but teacher expectations for the bright, average, and slow students may vary substantially.

Skill grouping within individual heterogeneously grouped classrooms. A first-grade teacher who divides the readers in her heterogeneously grouped classroom into smaller groups based on specific skill needs is using this grouping pattern. Subgroups, usually in math and language arts, are formed within the larger classroom to create a mix of skill-group and whole-group instruction with the teacher giving short lessons to each of the smaller groups. The instruction is modified to varying degrees for each of the groups. These groups are somewhat flexible in nature and are designed to meet specific skill needs for the short term.

Joplin Plan grouping across multiple grade levels. This plan groups learners who have the same skill level across two or more grades; it is flexible and allows for frequent assessment of student skill levels. Joplin grouping is primarily used for math and language arts classes where student learning is based on sequential skills (i.e., a child needs to know how to fluently subtract with borrowing before learning how to compute long division problems that require that subskill). Students in a school that uses Joplin grouping most commonly receive their instruction in subjects other than language arts and math in mixed-ability groups. A school implementing this approach has all of the fourth and fifth graders receive their math instruction at the same time of day with each student's assigned class determined by his or her math skill level. Each math class consists of a combination of fourth and fifth graders working at the same skill level. Because group assignments are not permanent, teachers frequently retest all students to see if their performance warrants a group change. Slavin, Madden, and Dolan's (1996) *Every Child, Every School: Success for All* (1996) school improvement model uses the Joplin Plan to deliver reading instruction. They describe that "The students are assigned to heterogeneous, age-grouped classes with class sizes of about 25 most of the day, but during a regular 90 minute reading period they are regrouped by reading performance levels into reading classes of students all at the same level" (pp. 5-6).

Questions to Ask About Grouping

Once you have identified the grouping pattern(s) most commonly used in your school, ask the following questions:

1. Why does your school staff group students according to the current plan? Has the superintendent dictated the current arrangements? Did you inherit the current grouping plan? Do the configurations reflect your own design plan?

2. Do your teachers use the same grouping pattern for subjects with sequential skills (e.g., math, language arts, and foreign language) as with subjects where broader content allows for more variation in the teacher's instruction (e.g., social studies, science)?

3. If you made a chart of all the students in your school grouped into their 10:00 a.m. classes and then circled all of the frustrated students for whom the 80% Commandment is being violated, how many students would be circled? If you next circled all of the students who are experiencing the 100% Snore, how many students would be circled? If you marked an X over the names of the circled students who have presented unmanageable behaviors, how many students would be circled?

4. Is the rationale for your grouping pattern(s) based on any of the following grouping myths?

Grouping Myths

Myth 1: Research supports mixed ability grouping over similar ability grouping. After an exhaustive examination of research studies that investigated skill grouping, Harvard authors concluded that "We cannot find a single large-scale, well designed experiment that follows students over several years to evaluate the impact of skill grouping" (Mosteller, Light, & Sachs, 1996, p. 812). The few controlled field trials that have been conducted are dated and include few students. All of the studies except for one was conducted on students in seventh grade and above. No compelling evidence supports either side of this important issue.

Myth 2: Mixed ability grouping raises self-esteem for lower achieving students. The Harvard researchers were surprised to find that even in one study, which determined that mixed ability grouping was slightly more effective, the students in the mixed ability groups were less engaged with their learning as measured by how often they spoke in class. Students in skill grouped classrooms tended to contribute to class discussions more frequently than those students who were in mixed ability groups (Mosteller et al., 1996, p. 813).

The same authors reported that the noncognitive data from the skill grouping studies leaned in favor of skill grouping: "On student self-report measures, skill-grouped students produced higher scores than the whole-class groups, both for liking their school more and for the amount of self-perceived learning" (Mosteller et al., 1996, p. 810).

Myth 3: Mixed ability grouping raises achievement levels more effectively for lower-achieving students. Most educators agree that instruction for lower-achieving students should adjust for their instructional needs through appropriate modifications and adaptations. Although many teachers are able to make the extensive modifications and adaptations to the curriculum that are needed in a mixed ability group setting, more often than not the teacher does not have the time or expertise to plan for that critical piece of the equation. The existing research further confuses this issue because the majority of studies that examine ability grouping patterns either examined classrooms in which the same instruction and the same methods were used for all ability level groups or did not indicate if and how instruction and methods varied between the two groups.

Slavin et al.'s research on high school grouping patterns is most often cited in support of the effectiveness of cooperative learning mixed ability groups. Taking a closer look at the studies he included in his analysis, researcher Bonnie Grossen (1996) reports that Slavin's review eliminated the studies that involved delivering different instructional programs for students with differing abilities. "Most of the practical impact of achievement grouping would be expected to come from high level students taking courses that cover more advanced content. Any studies that would have detected this effect were excluded from Slavin's reviews" (p. 6).

More recently, Slavin et al. (1996) seem to have recognized the need for flexibility in grouping patterns in order to meet the needs of at-risk students. Their widely heralded school reform model, Success for All, includes a combination of grouping strategies that include (a) heterogeneous, age-grouped classes of about 25 students, (b) cooperative learning, and (c) a modified Joplin Plan as mentioned earlier.

> Regrouping [use of the Joplin Plan with as many as three different grade levels of students with similar reading levels together in one smaller-size reading class] allows teachers to teach the whole reading class without having to break the class into reading groups. This greatly reduces the time spent in seatwork and increases direct instruction time. (Slavin et al., 1996, p. 6)

Myth 4: Courts view ability grouping as discriminatory and mixed ability groups lead to a higher level of equity. In "How Should We Group to Achieve Excellence With Equity," Grossen explains that although the courts rendered an opinion against ability grouping in *Hobson v. Hansen* (1967, 1969), ability grouping was supported in the subsequent case of

▬ Hobsen v. Hansen	+ Marshall v. Georgia
• Grouping decisions were based on a measure of general ability.	• Grouping decisions were based on a combination of academic indicators, with the primary emphasis resting on the child's level of achievement in a basal series.
• Students were assigned to the same permanent academic track.	• Some schools grouped students by subject, with their assignment to high, medium, or low groups varying depending on the subject. Thirty-seven percent of the students changed levels over the course of 2 academic years.
• The grouping system was associated with unequal resources and no compensatory educational benefits.	• Greater individualization of instruction was achieved, especially at the lower ability levels.
• No evidence showed that ability grouping was having a positive effect on the learning of children in the lower tracks.	• Evidence indicated improved performance on the Georgia Criterion Referenced Test, *especially* for lower-performing Black and White students.

SOURCE: Grossen, B. (1996, pp. 2-30).

McEwan, E., & Damer, M. *Managing Unmanageable Students: Practical Solutions for Administrators.*
© 2000, Corwin Press, Inc.

FIGURE 7.1   Comparison of Landmark Legal Decisions Regarding Grouping

Marshall v. Georgia (1984, 1985). The *Marshall* court described the school district's ability grouping as preferable to mixed ability groups because it was "designed to remedy the past results of past segregation through better educational opportunity for the present generation of black students" (Grossen, 1996, pp. 2-3). These two cases were distinguished by four critical differences that led to the differential ruling (see Figure 7.1).

Given the scarcity of valid studies investigating grouping alternatives, it is not surprising that the Harvard authors determined that the lack of evidence prevented them from making conclusive grouping recommendations. Because they singled out the Joplin Plan as a grouping pattern that showed promise, especially for teaching reading (Mosteller et al., 1996), we have provided a snapshot of how this grouping pattern could be used to reduce unmanageable behaviors related to the 80% Commandment and the 100% Snore.

How Flexible Grouping Can Make a Difference

Jessie Hunn, the principal of Evergreen School, arranged for the four classes of second graders and four classes of third graders to have math, reading, and spelling scheduled at the same time every day so that the teachers could implement the Joplin Plan grouping pattern. She appointed Doris Stewart, an outstanding fourth-grade teacher as team leader and was able to delegate many of the coordination functions to this capable master teacher. Students' placement into one of the eight groups in math, reading, and spelling was determined by skill level in that subject; a student might be in a low-level math group, a middle-level spelling group, and a high-level reading group. At least once per month, students were given short skill tests as the basis for determining their subsequent group placement. Many students stayed in the same group month after month, but others moved up and down levels depending on their progress. A second grader who was in a lower-skill group for addition with carrying, might jump up two or three levels when the class moved on to measurement because of her higher-level skills in that area of math. Teachers of a midlevel group were always delighted when they would teach a skill so well that their group surpassed a higher skill-level group.

Many of the students in the lowest skill group had special education eligibility, so the principal hired Melanie Crawford, a teacher with certification in special education, to work with the students in each of the three classes who had the most difficulty. Ms. Crawford's group had the fewest students in order to provide more intense support. The principal budgeted for a clerical aide who helped the teachers organize the skill tests, assisted with grading, and prepared materials. The teachers established a rotation system of testing the students' skills with the aide coordinating all the grading and related paperwork. Because the teachers brought in a student teacher each semester, they were also able to form another group, and so reduce the number of students assigned to each teacher.

In this flexible environment, gifted students were challenged and students at the lowest levels received intensive instruction geared to their level. The teachers used mixed ability grouping for all of the other subject areas they taught, individualizing for the different student levels when necessary.

Katina is a third grader who moved to Evergreen School recently. Last year, Katina's disruptive behaviors forced the school team to consider labeling her as behavior disordered. Under the Joplin Plan, Katina was able to receive the beginning-level reading and spelling skills she needed to be successful. In the small reading class taught by Melanie Crawford, Katina worked with a small number of students who were still learning to decode text fluently. As a result of this intense daily instruction with Ms. Crawford, she raised her reading level almost 1 year in only 5 months. Katina, who was a math whiz, worked with the highest-level skill class during that time and was challenged by the advanced fraction problems the group solved together. She initially had to move back a skill level during the geometry module, but in all of the other math areas she repeatedly tested into the highest group.

Because Katina could not independently read the third-grade social studies text, the teacher adapted the materials for the small group of students who required those changes. Because the students self-selected their favorite science topic for 4-week modules, Katina was currently in the "reptiles" class, her favorite subject of the day. The science teacher, who coincidentally also taught Katina social studies, had made a pact with her that if she remembered to raise her hand during the social studies' discussions she could feed the lizard at the end of science class. Although Katina's teachers agreed that Katina was one of their more challenging students, they no longer felt that a behavior disorder program was appropriate.

Fine-Tune Instructional Strategies

Grouping is not the only way you can reduce frustration and boredom. A second way is to help teachers develop highly motivating instructional strategies. Building these strategies into the repertoire of every teacher in your school will help to ensure that your students are on-task rather than in trouble.

Common sense dictates that the more time that an unmanageable student is on-task and actively participating in class-answering questions, completing work, writing information, or listening to the teacher's discussion, the less likely he or she will engage in unmanageable behaviors. Because a teacher's use of instructional strategies to increase on-task behavior is directly correlated with student behavior, determine whether these strategies are routinely used in classrooms where a student exhibits disruptive behaviors. The teacher who consistently uses these techniques will not only increase the time on-task of the disruptive student, but also of all the other students in the class. Here are some ways that teachers can adapt their instruction to maximize their students' time-on-task.

A Variety of Learning Tasks

Provide a variety of learning tasks during the class period. A longer lesson that is divided into shorter subsections with frequent activity changes will keep students more involved. Whether the lesson is 45 minutes of math manipulatives or 45 minutes of lecture, the results will be the same: a higher rate of disruptive behavior. Frequent activity changes with organized transitions are the key for holding all students' attention, especially a student with unmanageable behaviors. If Mr. Shook arranges instruction for his fifth-grade social studies class into the following schedule, all students are more likely to follow his rules and be actively engaged in the lesson:

1. First review the two new vocabulary words from the previous day's lesson (tribunal, defray) and ask some review questions to ensure that the students remember the material.

2. Conduct prereading activities with students for the day's assigned reading section on New Netherlands.

   a. Review any difficult-to-decode words and teach the new vocabulary words from the current day's reading (proprietor, generalization, patroon, and Stuyvesant).
   b. Discuss chapter headings and subheadings.
   c. Give each student a concept map with empty circles representing the sequence of events. Students will write two or three words about the major events in the empty circles on their concept maps as teacher highlights his completed concept map flashed on the overhead projector.

3. Switch to 10 minutes of guided reading during which students read aloud a section of the text about Henry Hudson and Peter Stuyvesant. Interject frequent questions related to the reading.

4. Instruct students to work together with a partner for 10 minutes to complete a graphic organizer grid asking for specific information about Henry Hudson and Peter Stuyvesant (who, what, where, and when). Students can use their books to help them locate the information.

5. Ask a few of the students to explain their completed grids before starting another 10 minutes of guided reading. Interject frequent questions related to the reading.

6. Give students instructions for homework that is due the next day. The homework assignment requires students to write a paragraph comparing Peter Stuyvesant's leadership with that of Roger Williams.

In *Every Minute Counts: Making Your Math Class Work* (Johnson, 1982), a veteran teacher describes another type of daily instructional plan that capitalizes on frequent activity changes to maintain a high level of student attention. Although the author writes about mathematics instruction, his recommendations apply to any subject matter. During the first 5 minutes of his class, this teacher launches into a quick homework review, a short basic skill practice, a challenging puzzle related to the previous day's work, or a readiness check. The math instruction that follows is characterized by a "ping pong" delivery of teacher explanation and example, always followed by student problem solving. The few minutes near the end of class are always reserved for giving the homework assignment before the teacher concludes with a final activity that might be a "challenge problem" or a set of practice problems given to teams of students.

Structured Choices

A second motivating instructional strategy is choice. Students will be more on-task and spend less time in disruptive behavior in a classroom where the teacher allows them to choose more of their learning activities (Munk & Repp, 1994). By planning structured choices during the day's lesson, a clever teacher can capitalize on this powerful motivator. In the social studies lesson described above, Mr. Shook could have asked his students whether they wanted to complete the graphic organizer grid with partners or independently. He could have presented students with a choice of four other colonial leaders with whom they could compare Peter Stuyvesant for the homework assignment. On another day, Mr. Shook might have given his students a choice either to put their comparisons on an overhead or to verbally present them, but because he wanted everyone to have more practice writing error-free paragraphs, he did not present that option for this lesson. The next day Mr. Shook might plan to have the class review the chapter and choose a game like Jeopardy or Blackboard Football to provide more motivation for extended practice.

Sometimes Mr. Shook allows students to choose whether they want to read the text silently or aloud, but because he has two poor readers, on those days he has to be prepared with taped text, two tape players, and headphones from the learning center for those students. Mr. Shook knows that bored students who complete their work before the others can present problems, and so he expects all students to bring a favorite book they are reading to his class. The students know that if their work is completed before others have finished, they may read.

Keep Things Moving

A third strategy is to maintain a fairly rapid pace to lessons that include many opportunities for students to respond during the class. The MTV generation that has grown up with lightning speed changes of action-packed scenes will be more off-task for any teacher whose instruction does not proceed at a lively pace. Downtime in the classroom soon dissolves into note-passing, back-poking, and insults. The student with unmanageable behaviors whose ability to wait is minimal will likely be the first to slide into off-task behavior while the teacher is across the room wasting precious moments taking the science equipment out of the cupboard or putting grades into the book. Unless materials are organized, questions preplanned before the lesson begins, and transitions brief and orderly, a teacher unwittingly provides opportunities for the more challenging student to engage in one or more of the problem behaviors identified in Chapter 1.

Teachers can ensure a lively pace by expecting all students to respond regularly. Frequent questions posed throughout instruction increase students' active thinking thereby increasing the time on-task. Mr. Shook requires that his students keep a paper and pencil on their desks during discussions, because he frequently pauses after one of his questions and asks everyone to write the answer before he calls on someone to give an oral response.

Teachers often use cooperative group work to involve students more actively, but the groups present their own unique challenges to maintaining high levels of student involvement. Whenever students in a cooperative group gossip about friends and social issues or let one student do the work for the entire group, on-task behavior decreases as does the opportunity for all students in the group to be actively involved in work. Because monitoring cooperative group work is more of a challenge than monitoring individual work, the teacher must move around the room at the speed of light, ears attuned, and eyes fixed on the rearview mirror. To ensure that all students are participating equally in a small group setting, the teacher can assign shorter structured tasks that do not violate the 80% Commandment nor produce the 100% Snore. If students know that the teacher will collect their cooperative group work product to see observable effort from all students and return the work with feedback within a day or two, they will be more likely to participate actively. Some teachers ask students to fill out checklists rating their role in the group effort at the end of a cooperative group activity. These ratings are beneficial because groups receive a higher rating if members indicate a high level of participation from everyone. Because honest evaluation of individual student effort is critical for this strategy to work, teachers need to closely monitor so that students' ratings match their performance.

Use Effective Teaching Sequences to Maximize Learning

Use effective teaching sequences to reduce student frustration and maximize learning. Success is the most powerful motivator for any student. A student's motivation to put forth maximum effort into a class increases whenever a student leaves the classroom with some knowledge or skill that he or she did not have at the start of the class.

Years ago, when one of the authors was working with violent teens in a youth facility, a more experienced teacher gave this wise advice: "If young people recognize that you have taught them something of worth, you will gain their respect. They may still tend toward violent behavior, but it won't be directed at you." She was right on. Not only did this advice provide the underpinnings for a productive, aggression-free experience, but later in other schools and other classrooms, applied to students of all ages and backgrounds.

The following teaching sequence (Archer, 1995) should decrease problem behaviors from your more challenging students and increase the percentage of time all students are on-task and learning productively.

Effective Teaching Sequences

An effective teaching sequence can last for several days or for only a few minutes but, depending on the type of lesson, it might include the following sequence: I Do It, We Do It, You Do It, Apply It.

Step 1: I Do It. The teacher demonstrates. For example, Mrs. Longo introduces the new sound for the letter *p* by showing the letter to the students and saying it for them. She then stops to ask herself this critical question: "Are the students ready to move on to Step 2?"

Step 2: We Do It. The teacher and students do the activity together with immediate feedback from the teacher. For example, Mrs. Longo practices saying the *p* sound together with the students. If students say the sound incorrectly, she assists them so they say it correctly. She then stops to ask herself: "Are students ready to move on to Step 3?"

Step 3: You Do It. The student does the activity independently and the teacher gives feedback about how the student did. This step is a practice phase with the teacher still involved. For example, Mrs. Longo asks the students to look at the *p* sound and read it out loud. She then has the students read words in which the students already know all of the letters except for the newly learned *p* sound. She then stops to ask herself: "Are the students ready to move on to Step 4?"

Step 4: Apply It. The student applies the skill to a novel problem, cooperative group activity, or real-life situations. For example, Mrs. Longo has students play the "Oh, No" game where a letter sound is called out. Students point their thumbs down if it is not the sound for *p*. Their thumbs go up in the air whenever a *p* is called out. Several days later, she will have students spell words that contain the letter *p*. Students are assigned to find two pictures of things or people in a magazine at home that begin with the letter *p*.

An Ineffective Teaching Sequence

Let's observe a lesson that failed as revealed by a student's unmanageable behaviors. Then we will determine how closely the example follows the effective teaching sequence to determine how the lesson should have been taught to maximize learning.

The third-grade teacher, Ms. Hextel, has just introduced division with remainders. First she gave the students manipulatives so they could divide them into a specified number of piles. This was a familiar activity to the students and she chose it as a review because she wanted them to connect it to the more abstract work they would do today.

After a few practice problems with the blocks, she moved into the "I Do It" phase of instruction and turned everyone's attention to the overhead while she demonstrated how to work 2 division problems such as 21 divided by 5. She then asked the students to complete a worksheet with 10 of these problems. Instruction then transitioned to the "You Do It" phase. Four minutes after the students began working on the worksheet, Alan turned around in his seat and fiddled with some papers on the desk of the girl behind him. Soon he was out of his seat, walking an exaggerated clown-walk to the pencil sharpener, pausing at a few boys' desks and drumming on the surfaces. Some of the boys were irritated, others seemed glad to stop working on their papers. On the way back to his desk, Alan flicked a rubber band at Cara. The entire class had now stopped working to watch the show.

What Went Wrong?

You have no doubt noticed that Ms. Hextel left out the "We Do It" phase of instruction that would have given the students direct practice and ensured a higher accuracy rate when they began working without her assistance. Alan, whose threshold for frustration was low, was unable to sit for one more minute in front of a worksheet filled with problems he could not solve independently. Any classroom can become chaotic within minutes if one or more student's accuracy rate dips below 80%. Other students who experienced frustration identical to Alan's were delighted to support his disruptive effort because it rescued them from the frustration of the task as well.

Ms. Hextel showed the students only two example problems at the overhead before expecting them to complete similar problems on their own. If she had posed a third problem to the class and quickly checked their answers, she would have seen that more than half of the class still needed help. She could have allowed the students who solved the problem to work ahead on the worksheet with the understanding that they would read their books quietly when they finished. Then she could have worked more sample problems with the students who needed additional help. Until these students could solve the problems with her at an 80% accuracy level, they could not be expected to solve them on their own. Only those students whose parents could teach them at home would be able to complete the worksheet as homework.

Think about a computer course you have taken in which the instructor left out the "We Do It" phase. The teacher no doubt began the course by passing out handouts containing information on how to design a Web site or how to set up a spreadsheet followed by an explanation of what to do. Sometimes the teacher might have students watch him or her move quickly through the software program before letting them work at an individual terminal. Some learners can profit from this type of learning situation, especially if they already have a high level of knowledge, but the majority of us cannot. We will leave the computer class still unable to design our own Web sites or put the budget equations into the district spreadsheet. We are too polite to act out, as are most adult learners, and so we choose either not to return to the class or quietly endure the frustration. Had the computer teacher taken us through the process step-by-step and given us the opportunity to practice, answering questions when our computer screen went blank or our numbers turned into asterisks, we would have avoided all the frustration that accompanies an unsuccessful learning experience.

What Is the Learning Quotient in Your School?

Determining If Your Classroom Environments Are Maximizing Learning

Charting off-task behavior is a relatively simple way to determine the effectiveness of the learning environments in your school. Staff members can benefit from knowing what percentage of the time a student with unmanageable behaviors is on-task compared with the rest of the students. Sometimes the results will surprise both them and you. For example, a teacher might single out a student as the source of classroom disruption when in reality three or four students are contributing to the problem. Unless the plan to resolve the problem involves the other students, it is doomed. Sometimes the student identified as unmanageable actually has a higher on-task rate than the majority of students in the class. In these rare instances, a teacher typically has discipline problems with the entire class but has unfairly targeted a minority student, the loudest student, or the tallest student as the source of the disruption. The student described as unmanageable seems to be the first face this teacher notices when scanning the classroom chaos.

Another key piece of information to obtain is whether the student with unmanageable behaviors is unable to stay on-task consistently or just intermittently. If Ines, a fifth grader, is on-task 90% of the time in language arts and science, but is on-task only 45% of the time in math class, look closely at the different environments in each of those classes. Are the science and language arts teachers more structured than the math teacher? Is Ines having more difficulty in the morning when compared with the afternoon? Are other students encouraging Ines's off-task behavior in math class? Has the 80% Commandment been violated in the math class? Because the data reveals that Ines has the capability to follow rules and remain on-task in language arts and science, what is going wrong in math?

In contrast, the fourth-grader Shauna was on-task between only 30% and 50% of the intervals during all observation periods. When Shauna finally started working on the appropriate schoolwork, she stayed on-task for 1 or 2 minutes before another distraction interfered. This consistently low on-task data suggests that resolving the problem that staff members have with Shauna will likely be more difficult than with Ines. Shauna's pattern is typical for children whose attention span is limited and for whom instruction may have to be specially adapted.

Expect to see a 90% on-task rate in any smoothly functioning classroom where students are learning and following the classroom rules. The percentage may dip down to 80% to 85% in a special education classroom or in any classroom when students are doing independent written work. On-task rates dip slightly during writing activities because writing is one of the most stressful activities in a classroom. Even when students are writing in journals without teacher expectations for an error-free product, the on-task rates dip slightly. Classrooms where on-task behavior consistently plummets below 80% need help immediately. In such poorly managed classrooms, not only is the academic work of all students compromised, but spending a year in such a classroom in the early grades may lead more difficult students to have higher rates of misbehavior 5 years later. In a study following 680 first graders, researchers found that aggressive, disruptive first graders who were in poorly managed classrooms were 59 times more likely to be aggressive in later grades. Aggressive, disruptive first graders who were in well-managed classrooms were only 3 times as likely to be aggressive in later grades (Kellam, 1998). A consistent discrepancy in the percentage of time on-task between the class sample and a student with unmanageable behaviors is an indication that your team should plan a formal behavior plan from the start. There are no hard and fast rules about the discrepancy in percentage of time on-task between the class sample and a student with unmanageable behaviors, but the authors' experience is that when the discrepancy is consistently more than 20%, resolving the problem will be more challenging and require more adaptations.

How to Collect On-Task Data

Collect on-task data by completing the Momentary Time Sampling Form (Form 2.4). Momentary Time Sampling provides the most accurate estimate of the percentage of time that a student is on-task for the following reasons:

1. On-task behavior is not readily countable.

2. One cannot readily determine when on-task behavior begins or ends.

3. On-task behavior often lasts longer than a few minutes.

You can most easily determine whether a student is on-task when you can see the student's face and eye movements, so plan to sit where you have a clear frontal view. As with all Momentary Time Sampling (MTS) data, record a "+" sign if the student is on-task at the exact instant the 10-second interval ends. Depending on the teacher's rules for the classroom, use our definition for on-task behavior that follows, adapt it, or write your own:

> The student is on-task if he or she is working, sitting in his or her seat or specified area, and behaving according to the teacher's rules and directions. The student's eyes should be focused on the teacher, on another student who has permission to talk, on the student's own school materials, or on instructional materials related to the lesson. If the student is talking, the conversation should be on topic (e.g., asks a question, answers a question, or participates in discussion).

The person taking on-task data will need to know the teacher's classroom rules to determine whether a student's action is on-task or off-task. Does the teacher allow students to blurt out answers or is hand raising required? Are students free to get required materials or sharpen a pencil at any time or are those functions only allowed before and after instruction? Although following active eye movement is usually the most accurate way to determine on-task behavior, occasionally you will take data on a student who shuts out the ongoing visual field as a strategy when concentrating on what the speaker is saying. Such students will routinely shut their eyes or turn their heads and stare at a spot during discussions. Because these students actively answer questions and complete the work, the teacher knows that they are on-task. You will not encounter this situation often, but when you do, alter the on-task definition to fit the situation so that your marking the student on-task does not depend on following his or her eye movement.

To obtain an on-task percentage for a student's peers in the classroom, randomly select six students in the class whom you can see clearly and who represent a random sample of the class. Try to select three female and three male students who represent the diversity of academic levels and behaviors in the class. Write each of their names in the boxes above the 10-second intervals on the MTS data form. Exhibit 7.1 shows a completed data form from an observation in which the data taker looked at Crystal when the first 10-second time interval ended, marking that she was

Student: **Six students in classroom**
Date: **4/13**
Teacher: **Greta Jacoby**
Setting: **Fourth Grade Language Arts**
Activity: **Independent Work at Desks**
Behavior: **On Task**
Start Time: **11:20**
Stop Time: **11:30**

Key: +   Behavior occurred at the <u>end</u> of the interval.
        -    Behavior did <u>not</u> occur at the end of the interval.

	Crystal	Simone	Paul	Kyle	Sheree	Andrew
Minutes	10"	20"	30"	40"	50"	60"
1	+	-	+	+	+	+
2	+	+	+	-	+	+
3	+	+	+	+	+	+
4	+	+	+	+	+	+
5	+	+	+	+	+	-
6	+	+	+	+	+	+
7	+	+	+	+	+	+
8	+	+	+	-	+	+
9	+	+	+	+	+	+
10	+	-	+	+	+	-

Number of intervals where behavior occurred x 100 = percent of occurrence
          Total number of intervals

54/60 x 100 = 90% of occurrence : On Task
Representative: (Y) N

EXHIBIT 7.1 Completed Momentary Time Sampling Data Form

on-task at that second. After another 10 seconds had elapsed, the data taker marked that Simone was not on-task before transferring attention to Paul who was observed as on-task when 30 seconds had elapsed. When the data taker finally marked that Andrew was on-task at the 60-second interval, she started once again with Crystal who was again on-task, proceeding in this round robin format working across the page and then down, until the 10-minute sample was complete.

Because monitoring student behavior when observing cooperative work groups is more challenging, do not attempt to assess students in more than one cooperative group at a time. You will obtain more accurate data if you watch two or three students in one group for 10 minutes and then watch students in a different group for another 10 minutes. If you are taking data on two students, write their names (e.g., Kayla, Bela, Kayla, Bela, Kayla, Bela) across the top of the page. Move from left to right across the page and record an observation every 10 seconds, first looking at Kayla, 10 seconds later at Bela, 10 seconds later back to Kayla, and so on until the 10 minutes are finished. If you can write a word or two identifying the off-task behavior when you mark it, you will have even more information about what the students are doing while off-task. The on-task data should be added to your other data and used for communicating the current problem to parents as well as for providing assistance to your team for planning. When talking to the parent or describing the data to the team, the principal might report the following:

> I observed Theresa in Mr. Hunter's classroom on 2 different days. During the first morning I observed her for 10 minutes and then watched her peers for another 10 minutes. [At this point the principal included a brief explanation of the MTS sampling process and explained how he randomly chose the six peers. He also displayed the chart to the members of the group.]
>
> During the first 10 minutes of a discussion in math class, Theresa was on-task 80% of the time while her peers were on-task 87% of the time. There was no significant difference between her behavior and that of her peers. Theresa's most frequent off-task behavior was talking out. Her peers' most frequent off-task behavior was almost always glazed eyes looking away from the teacher.
>
> Three days after the first observation, I watched Theresa work on an independent writing project in language arts class where she was on-task 63% of the time. In contrast, her peers were on-task 88% of the time. Theresa teased the boy sitting in front of her, thumped her pencil on his back several times, drew a picture rather than the assigned paragraph, and danced to the pencil sharpener three times. These behaviors contributed to her being significantly more off-task than her peers. Both teachers described Theresa's behavior as being representative of a typical day in their classrooms.

In the above example, the principal continued by concluding that the majority of Theresa's unmanageable behaviors were occurring in language arts class. The team was now ready to look at the dynamics that might be triggering Theresa's behavior in that classroom to brainstorm possible modifications and to implement the plan. Problem solved? Case closed? Not quite, but the team members will more likely be successful in their endeavor because they recognize the critical relationship between academic success and behavior. They know exactly what is happening to Theresa during instruction and are working as a team. The principal has some additional supervisory/evaluative work to do as a result of his observations in Theresa's mathematics class. The off-task behavior exhibited by the entire class is a much larger problem than merely working with Teresa. Obviously, the mathematics teacher will benefit from assistance in fine-tuning her instructional strategies and stepping up the pace of instruction so that all students, including the targeted student, are on-task.

The Challenge Is Yours

As an instructional leader, you have a responsibility to maximize learning for every student in your school, but doing it for a student with potentially disruptive behavior tendencies brings the following multiple benefits:

1. The achievement of all students is likely to improve in direct proportion to the increased time a teacher devotes to instruction as opposed to time spent dealing with unmanageable students.

2. Teacher morale and parental satisfaction are likely to increase.

3. Funds that would have been spent over time for special education placements, substitutes for discouraged and demoralized teachers, and added staff to compensate for students who repeat a grade can be allocated to other programs. "When one hour of class time per day is reclaimed for meaningful instruction, the savings per year are $23,249 per class, based on the national average cost per pupil of $5,623" (American Federation of Teachers, 1999, p. 2). For each student that an intervention keeps from having to repeat a grade, the savings are $5,623.

Just as important as the overall educational and economic benefits to be realized from these instructional initiatives are the emotional and psychological benefits that will accrue to each individual student whose daily experience at school becomes positive rather than negative.

CHAPTER EIGHT

The Proactive Principal

Fifty Things You Can Do Tomorrow

Managing unmanageable students requires a proactive approach. Here are 50 things that you and your staff members can do to create an environment of high expectations, success, and safety for all students.

1. ***Form a Crisis Team.*** Teachers should never have to subdue or move an unwilling student out of the classroom by themselves. In these times of increased litigation and escalating violence, every school—even elementary schools—should form a crisis team of at least four individuals who have taken a short training course designed to teach safe intervention techniques used with physically aggressive students. Crisis team members should always wear a pager during the school day, so that their immediate assistance is available to any staff member. A well-trained intervention team will prevent most disruptive situations from escalating into direct physical encounters and ensure that (a) the student does not harm self or others, and (b) staff members are not injured. Develop a board-approved written policy detailing how your school responds when the need for possible physical intervention arises. Include a plan for notifying parents about the intervention in writing. When you have identified a student receiving special education services who may at some point require physical intervention, always include details of how your school will respond in the student's current IEP. Two agencies that will provide crisis training either on-site or in various city locations are the following:

Crisis Prevention Institute (CPI)
http://www.crisisprevention.com/form.html
3315-K North 124th Street
Brookfield, WI 53005
1-800-558-8976

The Garrison Model Training
936 West Michigan
Jacksonville, IL 62650
217-245-7174

2. *"I Learned to Read Today."* The connection between disruptive behavior and lack of reading ability is a strong one. Identify nonreaders and
poor readers in your school, no matter what their age and provide immediate, intensive, daily reading instruction. Use programs that include a
phonemic awareness component: PhonoGraphix (McGuinness &
McGuinness, 1998), *The Writing Road to Reading* (Spalding, 1990), LiPS
(Lindamood Bell Learning Processes), or SRA Reading Mastery (Engel-
mann & Bruner, 1983). The lack of phonemic awareness skills is the single
best predictor of reading failure. It is never too late to learn to read, and
many students who have been diagnosed as behavior disordered or learning disabled simply have never had a teacher or a program in which they
experienced success.

3. *Arrange for Release Time for Classroom Visitation.* Allocate extra
money in your substitute teaching budget to release teachers for in-build-
ing or in-district observations of other teachers. Encourage Toni
Timewaster and David Disorganized to spend a half-day charting the
time-on-task percentages of previously unmanageable students in Sally
Structured's classroom. Offer Al Annoyed and Susan Short-Tempered the
opportunity to watch an unmanageable student in Melvin Mellow's classroom. Virtual reality can often be worth a thousand of your well-chosen
words.

4. *Provide Anger Management for Staff.* Provide a workshop for staff
members on how to defuse and manage their own anger. Purchase multiple copies of *Tongue Fu!* (Horn, 1996) or *How to Deal with Parents Who Are
Angry, Troubled, Afraid, or Just Plain Crazy* (McEwan, 1998b), and form
discussion groups. Help teachers learn to manage their own behavior so
they can do a more effective job of managing the behavior of challenging
students and their parents.

5. *Encourage Your Teachers to Let Go of the Past After Medication
Changes.* When a student starts taking a new medication or goes off the
old one, be optimistic about the potential for dramatic improvement. The
student whose aggression necessitated your calling in the police might return to your school as a mellow child once the Prozac™ medication is discontinued. The student with a history of verbal aggression toward teachers might return to school with the triggering depression under control
once Prozac™ is started. Not even a neurologist can be certain how any
specific student will respond to medication. Too often the student returns
to school a changed individual, but teachers still relate to the former

troublemaker. Be sure that students whose behavioral symptoms are finally alleviated medically get the second or third chance they deserve.

6. ***Get More Bang for Your Buck.*** If you hire a behavior consultant, appoint one or two individuals on your staff to shadow him or her during the time spent at your school. The social worker, psychologist, and special education teacher would be likely choices to benefit from this on-the-job training. These staff members should be involved in every aspect of the consultation from data collection to team meetings. Train your staff in the skills that are needed to function as behavior consultants for your school team. After working on two or three cases with the behavior consultant, they should be ready to take over.

7. ***Learn About Tourette Syndrome.*** Sometimes students who are viewed by the school as disruptive or as having an attention deficit disorder have Tourette syndrome that has not been identified. Teachers are apt to view these students' involuntary actions as purposeful and defiant. Although some students with Tourette syndrome will be outstanding students in your school and never require behavior intervention, others will need your staff's understanding of their condition as well as adaptations. Become familiar with issues related to Tourette syndrome through the Tourette Syndrome Association, Inc. (On-line.) Available: http://tsa.mgh. harvard.edu/. The Tourette Syndrome Association will provide or lend your school videos, movies, reading material, and speakers at no cost.

8. ***Teach Early Keyboarding.*** Identify all fourth and fifth graders who are still having difficulty with writing skills and teach them how to keyboard fluently. Too often we have heard the parental complaint, "His behavior problems ended in high school when they taught him to type. Why did they wait so long?" Until the life-changing keyboarding course, school staff ignored the stress and anger that was triggered for a small number of students by their labored, slow writing. Although the handwriting of a student who falls into this category may improve imperceptibly from grade to grade, the length of writing assignments and demands keeps increasing. Do not let these students limp along until they finally learn to keyboard. Once children reach the third grade, their hands are large enough to learn to type. Learning center volunteers can be taught to conduct short, daily typing lessons until the student types fluently. After the student learns to keyboard, he or she can use the classroom computer for longer assignments while still writing answers to shorter assignments. In addition to reducing the frustration resulting from writing, a distractible student's ability to work independently is often enhanced by completing written work at a computer screen. Your teachers may resolve several instructional problems in one fell swoop.

9. ***Learn About Attention Deficit Hyperactivity Disorder (ADHD).*** Many unmanageable students have ADHD. The strategies and interven-

tions that work well for students with ADHD can be used with challenging students of every type. Consult *The Principal's Guide to Attention Deficit Hyperactivity Disorder* (McEwan, 1998a) and *The ADHD Intervention Checklist* (McEwan, 1998c) for help in modifying instruction, curriculum, and classroom environment for any unmanageable student.

10. ***Include More Exercise.*** Physical exercise, especially total-body activities demanding heavy work from the muscles, can lead to decreased stress and increased relaxation. Exercise activities that can promote relaxation include jogging, weight lifting, horseback riding, martial arts, isometrics, and rope jumping. Encourage the student's parents to enroll him or her in a related after-school program. Arrange for an exercise reinforcer as a reward option. Start a before-lunch jogging or weight-lifting club for some of your most energetic students.

11. ***Coordinate With the Student's Physician.*** If the parents of an unmanageable student have a good working relationship with you, they are more likely to allow the school nurse to keep in close contact with the student's primary physician. If the doctor and parent receive timely information and descriptive data on the student's behavior at school as well as at home, everyone wins. Your staff will further benefit by staying abreast of the student's latest medication changes and potential side effects.

12. ***Respect Alternative Approaches.*** Respect the rights of parents to explore every treatment alternative. Parents, who are having as many problems at home as you are at school with the student who has unmanageable behaviors, may seek out answers from alternative health practitioners. Bear with them through this struggle and recognize that they are looking for answers just as you are. As long as the alternative health approach is not harmful to the child, respect the parent's choice to pursue it and do not add to their stress by demeaning their choice. One of the authors has been surprised several times when parent's identification of a food allergy resulted in dramatic change for their child after nothing else had worked.

13. ***Get Rid of the Wiggles.*** Many younger students have a difficult time keeping their bodies quiet for any appreciable length of time. Encourage teachers in primary classrooms to interject short, structured "stretch" times into the daily routine or when they notice that their group is getting wiggly. One or 2 minutes of structured stretches will increase everyone's alertness for the work ahead.

14. ***Be Alert to "Line-Up" Problems and Crowded Hall Discomfort.*** If you notice that a student's disruptive behavior predictably occurs in crowded passing periods or in long lines, avoid those triggers as much as possible. Some students who are more sensitive to noise and unexpected

touch will experience increased stress and anxiety in the midst of over-stimulating surroundings. Standing in the middle of a line often results in unexpected touch/jostling from either direction as does walking down a crowded school hallway. The more aware the student is about the source of these uncomfortable feelings, the more control he or she has over preventing them. If being positioned in the middle of the line, being jostled in crowded halls, or being in the middle of a large throng of students appears to upset Kevin, respect the physiological basis for his distress and communicate an alternative action that he can take to feel more comfortable. For example, if Kevin insists on being first in line, the teacher can say, "Kevin, I know you feel uncomfortable standing in the middle of the line because it's more noisy, but Jason is in charge of this line today. If you stand in the back of the line, there will be no one in back of you and it's much quieter. You can stay where you are or go to the back." A common adaptation for high school students who are bothered by crowded, noisy hallways is to leave the classroom 2 or 3 minutes before or after the other students in order to avoid those trigger times.

15. ***Offer a Course.*** Arrange to have a nearby university offer an intensive off-campus course on behavior management and discipline during the summer. Teachers who are reluctant to attend summer school will often sign up for a course if it is scheduled for whole-day or half-day sessions for a week or two on-site in the school district. One principal from a district where 40 teachers attended a behavior management course during the summer was delighted to return in the fall and see incentive charts and motivation programs infused throughout the school.

16. ***Know Thyself.*** Sometimes students have no idea that their behavior looks so silly or inappropriate until they see it in action. If a student habitually is off-task during science class, ask a volunteer to videotape the class so that later in the day with the teacher's help, the disruptive student can replay the tape, record data about his behavior, and then graph the number of occurrences. When the disruptive behavior is significantly reduced, the videotaping stops. Although videotape technology has been around for a long time, schools are only beginning to use it for enhancing discipline and self-awareness. Up until recently, the only department putting its recording equipment to good use was the sports department. Always check with your school attorney before putting a new videotape plan into action, but when you are working to bring order to chaotic hallways or a food-throwing lunchroom, a video recorder can provide valuable assistance.

17. ***Help Teachers Develop Creative Reinforcers.*** Buy two or three joke books for the teacher's library and suggest that teachers photocopy and cut the jokes into joke-for-the-day rewards that students can pick from a grab bag. Purchase an easy step-by-step cartoon drawing book that the

klutziest teacher can follow. Because drawing cartoons brings instant status, some of your students with unmanageable behaviors will work hard for the opportunity to receive a short 4- or 5-minute drawing lesson. Volunteer to host "lunch with the principal," with a few students once or twice a month so teachers can add this motivator to their bag of tricks.

18. ***Post Clearly Worded Rules in the Hallways, Bathrooms, and Lunchroom.*** Help teachers maintain consistency in monitoring students' behavior in the public areas of your school. If you present the school rules to students at an assembly at the start of the year, and teachers monitor and encourage students to follow those rules, you should immediately increase your school's civility quotient.

19. ***Apologize When You Have Goofed.*** All of us make errors with students, parents, and staff, and the best recourse is a direct, frank apology, expressing our regret. We only compound the initial error if we do not acknowledge our mistake. Although a principal or teacher can feel that giving an apology is a sign of weakness, in the long run that action will increase the other person's respect and trust for you.

20. ***Team Up With a Nearby University or Community College for Data Taking Assistance.*** Education and psychology professors are always looking for opportunities to have their students gain observation and data collection skills. Ask your school psychologist or social worker to put together a weekly schedule of times, dates, and places so that you can assign college students to teachers for additional help in collecting accountability data for a student with unmanageable behaviors.

21. ***Create a Quiet Work Area in Every Classroom.*** Help every teacher create a private work area in his or her classroom. One teacher might need an extra file cabinet to use as a divider, someone else might need an extra student desk, but with a little planning you can help all of your teachers arrange private work spaces in their classrooms. If teachers have planned for this arrangement from the first day of school, you can be assured that students who need a distraction-free place to complete work will have someplace to go.

22. ***Join the CEC Council for Children With Behavior Disorders.*** Membership in this reasonably priced organization will provide you with journals and newsletters that contain articles directly related to behavior management practices. You will find articles such as, "How to Defuse Confrontations" and "Substance Use and Its Prevention: A Survey of Classroom Practices" to share with your teachers. As an added benefit, the council will send you notices about workshops and conferences on behavior management in your area. You can join on-line at http://www.cec. sped.org/home.htm.

23. ***Schedule a Mini-Inservice to Introduce Relaxation Techniques.*** Teachers who are "quick triggers," escalating into fury at the drop of a hat, need to learn relaxation techniques they can use in the midst of a tense situation. One of the most effective ways to achieve this instant relaxation is through deep slow breathing or progressive relaxation where one learns to tense and release various muscle groups throughout the body. You will assuredly put some of your staff to sleep if you schedule an inservice to teach relaxation, but you will give others some practical tools to stay calm in the face of tension-filled situations.

24. ***Train Your Staff to Avoid and Defuse Disruptive Student Confrontations.*** Many confrontations with students begin when a teacher walks toward a student with a threatening demeanor. Arrange a mandatory inservice for your entire staff, training them in practical strategies to avoid and defuse confrontations with students. When your staff learns to recognize the first signs of agitation and apply strategies to calm down a student before he or she escalates into disruptive behavior, you will reduce the number of crisis situations in your building. If and when a crisis does occur, staff who have learned the rules to defuse a confrontation and who have practiced those rules in simulated situations are more likely to prevent an escalation of violence.

25. ***Teach Students How to Self-Monitor.*** Self-monitoring interventions can be instructive and motivating for students. Teach a student to self-record each time he or she talks out, is noncompliant, or leaves the desk area. Each time Lynette talks out, she puts a tally mark in the chart taped to her desk. If this self-monitoring program is combined with a DRO program where Lydia earns points for not talking out, the teacher may see a rapid decrease in the behavior.

26. ***Establish a Parenting Resource Library.*** Be prepared to provide assistance when parents ask you for resources to help them with their difficult child at home. Your assistance can open the door to a solid partnership with these parents, and you will have more success later if you are working as a team from the start. Maintain a small library of practical parenting books that parents can use as resources, and at least once a semester arrange for an evening class on parenting skills. Get the word out to all your parents by advertising these resources in the school newsletters and on a bulletin board in the school. A suggested list of titles to get your library started can be found in Appendix C.

27. ***Plan Thoroughly for Crisis Situations.*** In today's society, any and every crisis situation can jolt you into action—a student experiences a psychotic break at school, becomes suicidal, or is kicked out of the home by foster parents who have had enough. Key ingredients for meeting the challenge posed by these crisis situations are the following:

1. A well-defined school district discipline plan

2. Identification of community resources

3. A solid working relationship with community agencies

4. A good relationship with student's parents

How well your school handles these crisis situations will depend on how proactive you have been and how much legwork staff members have done before the crisis to identify and locate resources. A savvy social worker or psychologist will be a vital link when you find yourself wondering what to do and who to call as the crisis unfolds. If your social worker or psychologist already has close links with key agencies in the community and has identified all the available options, you will save hours when a crisis arrives. The staff of a psychiatric hospital with whom you have worked closely in the past is more likely to find a spare bed, even when their rooms are filled. A county crisis intervention team with whom your social worker has maintained a relationship can provide invaluable help at your school site if immediate crisis services are needed. Throughout the crisis, the relationship you have previously developed with the student's parents will be key. From the start of any crisis, work hand-in-hand with those parents. The parents may be facing a frightening decision whether to hospitalize their child for drug rehabilitation or psychiatric monitoring. The police may be involved if the student has a discipline code violation that requires their intervention. The last thing you need is a set of angry parents storming into the office as adversaries. (A special thanks to Sue Workman, principal of James R. Wood Elementary School, Somonauk, Illinois, and David Wilson, associate principal of Tinley Park High School, Illinois, for their contributions to this section.)

28. *Form a Locker Squad.* Identify a group of individuals to serve as your school's locker squad. The squad might include one teacher from every team, several hall monitors, and the special education teachers. The locker squad members will have the responsibility at the end of the day to meet disorganized students at their lockers and ensure that they go home with the books and materials they need to complete homework assignments or to study for tests. Although you eventually want these students to develop the organizational skills needed to remember the needed materials independently, the locker squad can provide the crutch they initially need to help them remember homework assignment notebooks and textbooks.

29. *Schedule a Medication Inservice.* Did a student start displaying tics shortly after the Ritalin™ dosage was increased? Can asthma medication trigger hyperactive behaviors? Can anything be done if a seizure medication triggers lethargy in class? The more your staff members know about

the commonly prescribed medications and their potential side effects, the closer they can work in partnership with the parents and physician. Ask your nurse to develop a series of one-page information bulletins on medicines that have been prescribed for students in your building and issue an updated bulletin each month.

30. ***Bathroom Behavior Tips.*** Make use of the backs of the doors in female staff bathrooms to post quick behavior management tips, the one-page information bulletins about medication mentioned earlier, and creative ideas to use for classroom reinforcers. Post the same reminders over the men's urinals. Most staff members will take the few moments necessary to read information that might otherwise have been tossed or ignored. Make sure to keep the bathroom bulletins up-to-date and changing.

31. ***Use Homework Assignment Notebooks and Other Organizational Strategies.*** Helping a disorganized student get his or her act together can prevent unmanageable behaviors down the road, but teaching these skills requires a high degree of organization from the teacher. Teachers need to encourage and monitor organizational strategies for a few of their students in every class. Do some of the students need larger assignments broken into smaller segments with checkpoints for work completion? Does the teacher consistently use the homework assignment sheet, providing a minute or two at the end of class for completing it? Does the teacher provide a written one-page outline of requirements and a format for larger assignments? If the parents request a weekly progress monitoring form, does the teacher complete it and provide them with the information?

32. ***Blow Your Own Horn.*** Teach students with unmanageable behaviors to play a brass instrument. Controlled forceful blowing is a calming activity and can result in up to 4 hours of relaxation. See whether you can find an older volunteer to meet two or three of your most difficult students for music instruction. The group may sound out of tune, but if the students enjoy the attention and are more relaxed for the rest of the school day, the time has been well worth it.

33. ***Create a Human Rights/Discipline Committee.*** Take your school district discipline plan one step further and urge your superintendent to form an ongoing human rights/discipline committee. It will serve as an invaluable resource and protection for you and your team if membership reflects a cross section of professional and community views (e.g., physician, attorney, special educator, regular educator, university professor, parent, psychologist, board member, nurse, student, and community agency representatives). Serving as an advisory and monitoring group and meeting once every other month throughout the school year, this committee can hear selected case reviews, establish accountability guidelines, develop a

needs assessment, monitor parental consent status of behavior, provide information regarding legal implications of proposed behavior plans, and participate in the development and revision of discipline guidelines and procedures. Committee members should be expected to present mini-inservices over the course of the year on issues related to their area of expertise and to devote part of each meeting to giving opinions and related factual information to questions posed by district administrators. Once the committee is operational and functioning as part of the fabric of the district, you then have a forum to bring individual cases and questions about medical, ethical, or legal issues related to discipline.

34. ***Don't Sweat the Small Stuff.*** Naturally, you want all students in your school to meet high standards and be responsible for bringing the necessary supplies to class each day, but you will probably have to shelve that organizational goal for the student with unmanageable behaviors. First your staff must address the higher priority behaviors. Do not overwhelm the student by expecting too much all at once. Until the unmanageable behavior is no longer an issue, eliminate problems caused by disorganization and give the student access to materials he may have forgotten to bring to class. On a shelf in the classroom, the teacher can keep a jar of old, stubby pencils, discarded or lost pens, extra paper, and a spare set of textbooks. If teachers make and enforce a rule that only the borrowed paper leaves the classroom, they should not have to waste one more minute on the daily missing materials crisis.

35. ***Establish a Safe and Secure School Environment.*** Guarantee civility and a feeling of security in your school. Students cannot feel secure when they face bullying, ethnic slurs, or harassment during the school day. Establish consistent consequences for bullies, maintain an open door policy for student victims of bullies and their parents, and work together with your teachers to send a clear message that bullying and other forms of harassment will not be tolerated. You will want to check out the "Bullying in Schools and What to Do About It" website (at http://www.indigenet. unisa.edu.au/bullying/) to read practical tips and information about how schools around the globe are dealing with this problem.

36. ***Use the Personal Touch.*** Learn the name of every student in your school. If you have hundreds or even thousands of students, this may seem an impossible task, but come as close as you can to achieving it. Your personal touch will make students feel more connected to school and more responsible for their behavior. When school officials are nameless, faceless bureaucrats, it is much easier for students to break the rules.

37. ***Make a List and Check It Twice.*** Compile a list of every challenging or unmanageable student in your school. Make a point to stop in and visit their classrooms at least once or twice a week. If the teacher is not engaged

in direct instruction, make it a point to speak to the student in a warm and friendly manner. Address the student by name and give him or her a compliment. Check with the student's teacher ahead of time to determine an accomplishment about which you can commend the student. This practice will not only encourage and reinforce the student but will also hold the teacher accountable for focusing on the positives.

38. ***Find Your School's Danger Zones.*** Form student focus groups and ask them to look at maps of the school and point out the trouble spots—places where fighting, swearing, violence, and misbehavior typically occur. If your students respond as those in a recent study did, you will find out that all of these problems occur in locations where few or no adults are present: between class periods in hallways, cafeterias, gyms, auditoriums, and parking lots (Furlan & Viadero, 1999). Middle school students identified more danger areas than elementary students, due in part to the greater sense of ownership and responsibility for spaces outside their classroom expressed by elementary teachers as compared with middle school teachers. Increase adult supervision in the danger zones in your school and cultivate a sense of ownership and responsibility on the part of every staff member.

39. ***Be a Visible Presence.*** Where do you spend the majority of your working day? Behind closed doors or in classrooms, cafeteria, and the playground where you can greet students, observe teachers, and feel the pulse of your school? Your presence will not only let students know that you care but will remind those students who might be tempted to misbehave that it is not worth it. Visit as many classrooms every day as possible, even if you only drop in for a minute or two. Observe what is happening in classrooms with unmanageable students. Praise the teacher for her success with an intervention plan. Praise a student for the way in which he or she has turned around his or her grade point average.

40. ***Have an Open Door Policy.*** It is never easy to listen to criticism regarding one's school, but being responsive to student and parent concerns is one important way to reduce unmanageable student behaviors. You will know when a teacher's instructional effectiveness is sliding and have time to catch a problem before it becomes a full-blown emergency. You will have advance warning of problems at the bus stop or on the playground. Take time to investigate fully any complaints and then take steps to solve the problems.

41. ***Try Organizing a Lunch Bunch or Breakfast Club.*** Invite small groups of students to your office for breakfast or lunch. Encourage students to share the positives and the negatives of their schooling experience. Listen carefully to what they have to say relative to potential problems in your school. If students raise a concern, take the time to

investigate it and get back to the group with your findings and what you plan to do about it.

42. ***Be a Resource Provider.*** Strong instructional leaders find ways to provide resources for their staff members. When the special education teacher suggests an idea that will serve her students along with a dozen or more nonreaders in your high school population, find the money so she can do it. When your dean of students wants to develop a handbook of community resources, but needs a budget for printing expenses, locate the funds to get the job done. When an intervention plan requires extra computers for the classroom, call in a favor from the technology director. Your staff members will be willing to work twice as hard for you when you find the resources to help them meet the needs of students.

43. ***Clear Your Calendar.*** Be available for emergency meetings with staff regarding serious behavioral problems. Your consultation and involvement from the outset will often serve to prevent misunderstandings, due process hearings, and even lawsuits. Do not delegate the difficult jobs. Be there.

44. ***Develop a Building Discipline Plan.*** There is nothing more powerful than a building discipline plan developed and supported by every staff member. When all teachers feel responsible for the behavior of all students, the climate and culture of the school will no longer support rudeness, fighting, vandalism, and rampant rule breaking. Be prepared for some vigorous discussions over just which rules are most important and just what consequences are appropriate.

45. ***Clear Your Mind.*** Unmanageable students often enter the classroom with trouble already brewing. Their minds are whirling with frustration and anger. Some teachers have found it helpful to ask the student to make a list of everything that is on his or her mind and then lay it aside until after class. This process can clear the student's mind for studying or reading.

46. ***Create and Use Checklists for Common Classroom Assignments.*** Unmanageable students never seem to learn how to keep track of homework, what to do with assignments, how to write a book report, or how to write an essay. When teachers develop checklists for these common classroom assignments, the students can tape the lists to their desks, keep them in a notebook, or even refer to a posted list on a bulletin board.

47. ***Give Students Think Sheets.*** Develop sheets to be filled out by students after a behavior incident. These sheets force the student to think about behavior and then write about it. Sample questions include the following:

1. What did you do?

2. What were you supposed to do?

3. How will you handle the situation next time?

48. ***Extracurricular Involvement.*** Draw up a list of your most unmanageable students. Then determine what kind of extracurricular activity would best use that student's strengths and talents. See if you can facilitate the student's participation. In some cases, you may have to assign the task of resource procurement to the social worker if the activity requires an entry fee.

49. ***How Does Your School Rate?*** Is your school "friendly" to students who arrive on your doorstep with challenging behavior problems? To find out, complete the following checklist:

   a. Do the administration and staff members believe that all students can learn?

   b. Are the rules and expectations for behavior in the school clearly stated and consistently applied in all classrooms and learning areas?

   c. Are the consequences for breaking the rules swiftly and fairly administered to all students?

   d. Is the school well-ordered and structured?

   e. Does the school staff believe in positive reinforcement, incentive programs, and motivational activities?

50. ***How Does the Principal Rate?*** Here are the top 10 characteristics of principals who are most effective in working with unmanageable students. How do you rate?

   a. Do you run a tight ship with regard to discipline, structure, and organization?

   b. Do you know how to procure resources for materials, programs, and inservice training?

   c. Do you attend all meetings and staffings regularly and participate collaboratively in all decisions regarding unmanageable students?

   d. Do you listen to parents and their concerns?

   e. Do you think about and help to solve the problems of unmanageable students creatively by coming up with one more plan, one more idea, or one more incentive?

   f. Do you hold both teachers and students to high expectations?

g. Do you believe that all can learn (this includes teachers, students, and parents)?

h. Do you regularly spend time with students (in the cafeteria, on the athletic fields, and in the classrooms)?

i. Do you affirm, support, and encourage teachers?

j. Do you search out training opportunities for yourself to increase your knowledge and skills regarding how to help students with behavior problems become more successful in your school?

Conclusion

The relationship between authors and readers is a unique one. Although we may never meet face to face, we feel that you are our colleagues. You know exactly what we believe and where we stand on some very crucial educational issues. Our goal as educators is to maximize learning and success for every student, even the most unmanageable ones. When students can learn, their behavior will almost always improve. We received an e-mail not long ago from a special education teacher in Michigan that summarizes our philosophy eloquently.

Linda is an experienced high school special education teacher whose resource room contains some of her school's most unmanageable students—emotionally impaired, behavior disordered, and learning disabled—and she has found the secret to turning their behavior around: learning. Her biggest success story is Robert. This is the story she tells.

Robert's file is the thickest in the school because of his horrible behavior problems. Because I had taught his older brother, his parents requested that Robert be placed with me, but the principal refused because my caseload already contained "too many tough boys." Instead, Robert was sent to a behavior disorder class in a town more than 25 miles away. He seemed to do okay during the first year, but then an untrained teacher with no plan, no goals, and no skills was hired. Robert went ballistic and, in his own words, "flunked out" of the class for behavior problems.

There were no options. Robert had to be assigned to my class. This was when I learned the most important lesson of my entire teaching career (46 years, for I began tutoring my deaf brother when I was 5 years old). Before Robert arrived, I took his older brother, Johnny, aside and asked his opinion.

"Why do you think Robert acts so awful?" I asked.

He lowered his voice and said sadly, "I think that all Robert has ever wanted was to learn to read." Without a doubt, that sentence gave me more insight into children than all my years at university.

As soon as Robert arrived I took him aside. "I understand that you want to learn to read. It will not happen overnight, but I promise you that if you stick with me, I will teach you."

To date I have never had to discipline Robert in any way. The most I have had to do is gently remind him to stop chatting and save it for break time. And that is only rarely. He is reading *Danny, the Champion of the World* by Roald Dahl, a book I highly recommend to teachers working with reading remediation with teens. Robert is doing a study of the death of the rapper, 2Pac, has a theory, and is checking many sources. He just borrowed *The Prince* by Machiavelli from me as he thinks it may figure in the conundrum posed by the death of the rapper.

Robert is a source of inspiration to the other students in my class. Last year I presented Robert with a certificate of merit in front of the whole school. Robert also won a citizenship award from the administration—an honestly deserved one. Robert has served as a library aide this year; he couldn't even alphabetize when I persuaded my friend the librarian to work with him. Now the librarian hates to lose him. He had always dreamed of working in a library and being entrusted with books. That is Robert.

There is also Nellie—from one of the worst backgrounds one can imagine, and working hard to succeed at community college! I knew she had gotten over the hump, into the land of the readers, on the day she arrived at school breathless with her explanation of how she had "crawled right into the pet shop" of the book she was reading! She says I changed her life and even called me on Mother's Day to tell me she loves me.

Then there is Helen—the one whom everyone has hated and isolated since her days in elementary school. She arrived in my room tormented and harassed. She cried over every little thing and could barely read a word. I gave her love and phonics. Helen is now reading her way through the Laura Ingalls Wilder series. Each week her oral reading is smoother and she speaks of the characters as friends. We have a bet—she tries to hold back her tears and not let her tormentors push her buttons, and I pay for the Wilder books as fast as she can read them and give me an oral report. It turns out that she is a lovely, caring person. She would give away all of her possessions to help someone!

Why have students succeeded in my classroom? I teach differently from other teachers. I rarely use worksheets. I stand and talk! I follow the lead of Dr. Daniel Ling, famous teacher of the deaf who says that the best teaching will be done "with wee chats." I tell my students about life, my travels in Europe, my problems when I was a kid, how to set goals, and how to maintain one's personal dignity in a crazy world. We work on vocabulary and spelling constantly. We work on our reading program [*The Writing Road to Reading* by Romalda and Walter Spalding] in depth. The kids go home each night chattering to their parents that English does make sense, that there are rules, and that if you have a good think about the probable root of a big word, you can figure out the meaning! They are happy. They are planning for the future.

Linda was debating whether to stay in special education but, after sharing her story with Mary and me, she concluded that she would. The Roberts of her high school need her.

She concluded her message with these observations.

One more thought before I go. In hours of talks with Robert—he is now nearly a family member and spends much time with us—I believe I have gotten a peek into his mind to see what makes him tick. Here is what Robert and I have come up with to explain his prior behaviors. Each school year he arrived with high hopes, new pencils, and anticipation that this year would be different. This year there would be a teacher who would see that he desperately needed to learn to read. And each year, when he encountered the same frustration he became angry—again. Each time that Robert's teachers handed him a stack of worksheets with orders to "Do them!" he became enraged. Each time that teachers wrote on the boards, never stopping to think that he could not read cursive writing, and ordered him to "Take notes!" a bit of him died.

Are there any students like Robert, Helen, or Nellie in your school? Think about what you can do as an instructional leader to give them the gift of academic success.

Reference Tools
for Principals

Abrams, B., & Segal, A. (1998). How to prevent aggressive behavior. *TEACHING Exceptional Children, 30*(4), 10-15.

Acheson, K., & Gall, M. (1992). *Techniques in the clinical supervision of teachers* (3rd ed.). White Plains, NY: Longman.

Alberto, P., & Troutman, A. (1999). *Applied behavior analysis for teachers* (5th ed.). Englewood Cliffs, NJ: Prentice Hall Merrill Education.

American Federation of Teachers. (1996). Disruption, discipline and quality alternative placements. *Questline, 4*(1), 1-4.

Ayers, B., & Meyer, L. (1992). Helping teachers manage the inclusive classroom: Staff development and teaming star among management strategies. *The School Administrator, 49*(2), 30-37.

Bender, W., Clinton, G., & Bender, R. (1999). *Violence prevention and reduction in schools.* Austin, TX: Pro-Ed.

Braaten, S., Simpson, R., Rosell, J., & Reilly, T. (1988). Using punishment with exceptional children: A dilemma for educators. *TEACHING Exceptional Children, 20*(2), 79-81.

Broome, S., & White, R. (1995). The many uses of videotape in classrooms serving youth with behavioral disorders. *TEACHING Exceptional Children, 27*(3), 10-13.

Bullying in schools and what to do about it. (1998). [On line]. Available: http://www.indigenet.unisa.edu.au/bullying/

Cangelosi, J. (1991). *Evaluating classroom instruction.* White Plains, NY: Longman.

Canter, L. (1987). *Schoolwide positive activities: Ideas for reinforcing positive schoolwide behavior grades K-6.* Santa Monica, CA: Lee Canter & Associates.

Cartwright, C., & Cartwright, G. (1984). *Developing observation skills* (2nd ed.). New York: McGraw-Hill.

Clemes, H., & Bean, R. (1980). *How to discipline children without feeling guilty.* Los Angeles: ENRICH™ Education Division of Price Stern Sloan.

Colvin, G. (1997). How to defuse defiance, threats, challenges, confrontations. *TEACHING Exceptional Children, 29*(6), 47-51.

Council for Exceptional Children. (1997). *IDEA 1997 regulations* [On-line]. Available: http://www.cec.sped.org/idea/index.html

Council for Exceptional Children. (1997). *Strategies to meet IDEA 1997's discipline requirements* [On-line]. Available: http://www.cec.sped.org/bk/focus/1297.htm

Council for Exceptional Children. (1998). *Readings and resources on school discipline* [On-line]. Available: http://www.cec.sped.org/minibibs/eb20.htm

Daniels, V. (1998). How to manage disruptive behavior in inclusive classrooms. *CEC: Special Web focus* [On-line]. Available: http://www.cwc.sped.org

Dell, T. (1993). *Motivating at work: Empowering employees to give their best.* Menlo Park, CA: Crisp.

Drasgow, E. (1997). Positive approaches to reducing undesirable behavior. *Beyond Behavior, 8*(2), 10-13.

Dunlap, G., Kern, L., dePerczel, M., Clarke, S., Wilson, D., Childs, K. E., White, R., & Falk, G. D. (1993). Functional analysis of classroom variables for students with emotional and behavioral disorders. *Behavioral Disorders, 18*(4), 275-291.

Englert, C., Tarrant, K., & Mariage, T. (1992). Defining and redefining instructional practice in special education: perspectives on good teaching. *Teacher Education and Special Education, 15*(2), 62-86.

Evans, S., Evans, W., & Gable, R. (1989). An ecological survey of student behavior. *TEACHING Exceptional Children, 21*(4), 12-15.

Evans, W., Evans, S., Gable, R., & Kehlhem, M. (1991). Assertive discipline and behavioral disorders: Is this a marriage made in heaven? *Beyond Behavior, 2*(1), 13-16.

Foster-Johnson, L., & Dunlap, G. (1993). Using functional assessment to develop effective, individualized interventions for challenging behaviors. *TEACHING Exceptional Children, 25*(3), 44-50.

Fuchs, D., Fernstrom, P., Scott, S., Fuchs, L., & Vandermeer, L. (1994). Classroom ecological inventory: A process for mainstreaming. *TEACHING Exceptional Children, 26*(3), 11-15.

Grossen, B. (1996). *How should we group to achieve excellence with equity* [On-line]. Available: http://darkwing.uoregon.edu/~adiep/grp.htm

Johns, B. (1998). What the new Individuals With Disabilities Education Act (IDEA) means for students who exhibit aggressive or violent behavior. *Preventing School Failure, 42*(3), 102-105.

Johns, B., Carr, V., & Hoots, C. (1997). *Reduction of school violence: Alternatives to suspension.* Horsham, PA: LRP Publications.

Katsiyannis, A. (1995). Disciplining students with disabilities: What principals should know. *NASSP Bulletin, 79*, 92-96.

Katzenback, J., & Smith, D. (1993). *The wisdom of teams: Creating the high-performance organization.* New York: HarperCollins.

Klubnik, J., & Greenwood, P. (1994). *The team-based problem solver.* New York: McGraw-Hill.

Koorland, M., Monda, L., & Vail, C. (1988). Recording behavior with ease. *TEACHING Exceptional Children, 21*(1), 59-61.

Lewis, T. (1995). *Decision making about effective behavioral support: A guide for educators* [On-line]. Available: http://idea.uoregon.edu/~ncite/documents/techrep/tech25.html

McEwan, E. K. (1998). *The ADHD intervention checklist.* Thousand Oaks, CA: Corwin.

McEwan, E. K. (1998). *Leading your team to excellence: How to make quality decisions.* Thousand Oaks, CA: Corwin.

McEwan, E. K. (1998). *The principal's guide to attention deficit hyperactivity disorder.* Thousand Oaks, CA: Corwin.

McEwan, E. K. (1998). *Seven steps to effective instructional leadership.* Thousand Oaks, CA: Corwin.

Meyer, E., Vergason, G., & Whelan, R. (1988). *Effective instructional strategies.* Denver, CO: Love.

Mosteller, F., Light, R., & Sachs, J. (1996). Sustained inquiry in education: Lessons from skill grouping and class size. *Harvard Educational Review, 66*(4), 797-828.

Nelson, B. (1994). *1001 ways to reward employees.* New York: Workman.

Nelson, J., Crabtree, M., Marchand-Martella, N., & Martella, R. (1998). Teaching good behavior in the whole school. *TEACHING Exceptional Children, 30*(4), 4-9.

Nichols, P. (1993). Some rewards, more punishment: A look at application of behaviorism [Review of the book "Punished by rewards"]. *Beyond Behavior, 5*(1), 4-13.

Panico, A. (1998). *Discipline and the classroom community: Returning control of our schools.* Mequon, WI: Stylex.

Smith, C., & Laslett, R. (1993). *Effective classroom management: a teacher's guide.* New York: Routledge.

Sorenson, G. P. (1990). Special education discipline in the 1990s. *West's Educational Law Reporter, 62*(2), 387-398.

Sulzer-Azaroff, B., & Mayer, G. (1991). *Behavior analysis for lasting change.* New York: Holt, Rinehart & Winston.

Umbreit, J. (1995). Functional assessment and intervention in a regular classroom setting for the disruptive behavior of a student with attention deficit hyperactivity disorder. *Behavioral Disorders, 20*(4), 267-278.

Walker, H. (1979). *The acting-out child: Coping with classroom disruption.* Boston: Allyn & Bacon.

Weber, J., & Scheuermann, B. (1991). Accentuate the positive . . . Eliminate the negative! *TEACHING Exceptional Children, 24*(1), 13-19.

Williams, B., & Katsiyannis, A. (1998). The 1997 IDEA amendments: Implications for school principals. *NASSP Bulletin, 82*(594), 12-18.

Yell, M. (1988). The effects of jogging on the rates of selected target behaviors of behaviorally disordered students. *Behavioral Disorders, 13*(4), 273-279.

Yell, M. (1990). The use of corporal punishment, suspension, expulsion, and timeout with behaviorally disordered students in public schools: Legal considerations. *Behavioral Disorders, 15*(2), 100-109.

Yell, M. L., & Shriner, J. G. (1997). The IDEA Amendments of 1997: Implications for special and general education teachers, administrators, and teacher trainers. *Focus on Exceptional Children, 30*(1), 1-19.

Practical Tools for Teachers

Add these practical problem-solving books to your school's professional library. They will be helpful to your staff members as they seek to grow more skillful in meeting the needs of challenging students.

Albert, L. (1989). *A teacher's guide to cooperative discipline: How to manage your classroom and promote self-esteem.* Circle Pines, MN: American Guidance Service.

Bluestein, J. (1988). *21st century discipline.* Jefferson City, MO: Scholastic.

Cangelosi, J. (1993). *Classroom management strategies: Gaining and maintaining students' cooperation* (2nd ed.). New York: Longman.

Canter, L. (1987). *Positive reinforcement activities.* Santa Monica, CA: Lee Canter & Associates.

Canter, L. (1993). *Succeeding with difficult students: New strategies for reaching your most challenging students.* Santa Monica, CA: Lee Canter & Associates.

Canter, L. (1994). *Scared or prepared: Preventing conflict and violence in your classroom.* Santa Monica, CA: Lee Canter & Associates.

Curwin, R., & Mendler, A. (1988). *Discipline with dignity.* Alexandria, VA: Association for Supervision and Curriculum Development.

Emmer, E., Evertson, C. B., & Worsham, M. (1999). *Classroom management for secondary teachers.* Needham Heights, MA: Allyn & Bacon.

Fad, K., Patton, J., & Polloway, E. (1998). *Behavioral intervention planning.* Austin, TX: Pro-Ed.

Fister, S. L., & Kemp, K. A. (1995). *Making it work on Monday.* Longmont, CO: Sopris West.

Jenson, W., Rhode, G., & Reavis, H. (1996). *The tough kid tool box.* Longmont, CO: Sopris West.

Johns, B., & Carr, B. (1995). *Techniques for managing verbally and physically aggressive students.* Denver, CO: Love.

Johnson, D. (1982). *Every minute counts: Making your math class work.* Palo Alto, CA: Dale Seymour.

Kauffman, J., Hallahan, D., Mostert, M., Trent, S., & Nuttycombe, D. (1993). *Managing classroom behavior: A reflective case-based approach.* Boston: Allyn & Bacon.

Kameenui, E., & Darch, C. (1995). *Instructional classroom management: A proactive approach to behavior management.* White Plains, NY: Longman.

Kerr, M., & Nelson, C. (1989). *Strategies for managing behavior problems in the classroom* (2nd ed.). Columbus, OH: Merrill.

O'Shea, L., & O'Shea, D., & Rosenberg, M. (1998). *Student teacher to master teacher: A practical guide for educating students with special needs* (2nd ed.). Upper Saddle River, NJ: Prentice Hall.

Paine, S., Darch, C., Deutchman, L., Radicchi, J., & Rosellini, L. (1983). *Structuring your classroom for academic success.* Champaign, IL: Research.

Rhode, G. (1992). *The tough kid book: Practical classroom management strategies.* Longmont, CO: Sopris West.

Sprick, R. (1985). *Discipline in the secondary classroom: A problem-by-problem survival guide.* West Nyack, NY: The Center for Applied Research in Education.

Walker, H. (1991). *Coping with noncompliance in the classroom: A positive approach for teachers.* Austin, TX: Pro-Ed.

Watkins, K., & Durant, L. (1992). *Complete early childhood behavior management guide.* West Nyack, NY: The Center for Applied Research in Education.

Watson, G. (1998). *Classroom discipline problem solver: Ready-to-use techniques and materials for managing all kinds of behavior problems.* West Nyack, NY: The Center for Applied Research In Education.

Resource Library for the Parents of Elementary School Students

Purchase these books for your parent resource library. Recommend them to parents of elementary-age children who have difficult-to-manage behaviors.

Bateman, L., with Riche, R. (1986). *The nine most troublesome teenage problems and how to solve them.* New York: Ballantine.

Canter, L. (1985). *Parent resource guide.* Santa Monica, CA: Lee Canter & Associates.

Garber, S., Garber, M., & Spizman, R. (1987). *Good behavior: Over 1200 solutions to your child's problems from birth to age twelve.* New York: Villard.

Garber, S., Garber, M., & Spizman, R. (1990). *If your child is hyperactive, inattentive, impulsive, distractible: Helping the ADD/hyperactive child.* New York: Villard.

Holt, P., & Ketterman, G. (1988). *When you feel like screaming! Help for frustrated mothers.* Wheaton, IL: Harold Shaw.

Kurcinka, M. (1991). *Raising your spirited child.* New York: HarperCollins.

McCullough, B., & Monson, S. (1981). *Forty ways to get your kids to work at home.* New York: St. Martin's.

McEwan, E. K. (1995). *Attention deficit disorder.* Wheaton, IL: Harold Shaw.

McEwan, E. K. (1996). *"The dog ate it": Conquering homework hassles.* Wheaton, IL: Harold Shaw.

McEwan, E. K. (1996). *"I didn't do it": Dealing with dishonesty.* Wheaton, IL: Harold Shaw.

McEwan, E. K. (1998). *When kids say no to school: Helping children at risk of failure, refusal, or dropping out.* Wheaton, IL: Harold Shaw.

Nelsen, J., Lott, L., & Glenn, H. (1993). *Positive discipline A-Z: 1001 solutions to everyday parenting problems.* Rocklin, CA: Prima.

Phelan, T. (1990). *1-2-3-Magic!: Training your preschoolers and preteens to do what you want them to do* [Video]. Carol Stream, IL: Child Management.

Rosemond, J. (1990). *Ending the homework hassle: Understanding, preventing, and solving school performance problems.* Kansas City, MO: Andrews & McMeel.

Schaefer, C., & DiGeronimo, T. (1990). *Teach your child to behave: Disciplining with love, from 2 to 8 years.* New York: New American Library.

Schaefer, C., & Millman, H. (1981). *How to help children with common problems: From early childhood through adolescence—A uniquely practical, reassuring, and effective parenting guide.* New York: Litton.

Turecki, S., & Tonner, L. (1985). *The difficult child.* New York: Bantam.

Wyckoff, J., & Unell, B. (1984). *Discipline without shouting or spanking: Practical solutions to the most common preschool behavior problems.* Deephaven, MN: Meadowbrook.

References

American Federation of Teachers. (1999). *Alternative educational placements for violent and chronically disruptive students* [On-line]. Available: http://www.aft.org/lessons/three/altvio.html

Archer, A. (Speaker). (1995, July). *The time is now* [Cassette recording]. World Association of Direct Instruction 21st Annual Conference, Eugene, OR.

Berger, W. (1999, February). Lost in space. *Wired*, pp. 76-81.

Educational Testing Service. (1998). *Order in the classroom*. Princeton, NJ: Author.

Englemann, S., & Brunner, E. C. (1983). *Reading Master I and II: DISTAR reading*. Chicago: Science Research Associates.

Furlan, C., & Viadero, D. (1999, June 23). Research notes. *Education Week*, p. 38.

Grossen, B. (1996). How should we group to achieve excellence with equity? *Effective School Practices, 15*(2), 2-16.

Gunter, P., Shores, J. S., & Rasmussen, S. (1995). On the move. *Teaching Exceptional Children, 28*(1), 12-13.

Hanson, C. (1994, March 13). Working smart: Praise is an appreciable bonus that strengthens motivation. *Chicago Tribune*, p. 9.

Horn, S. (1996). *Tongue fu!* New York: St. Martin's.

Huizinga, D., Loeber, R., & Thornberry, T. P. (1991). *Program of research on the causes and correlates of delinquency: Urban delinquency and substance abuse*. Washington, DC: Department of Justice, Office of Juvenile Justice and Delinquency Prevention.

Individuals With Disabilities Education Act of 1997, Pub. L. No. 105-17 [On-line]. Available: http://www.ed.gov/offices/OFERF/IDEA.

Johns, B. H., Carr, V., & Hoots, C. (1997). *Reduction of School Violence: Alternatives to suspension*. Horsham, PA: LRP Publications.

Johnson, D. (1982). *Every minute counts: Making your math class work*. Palo Alto, CA: Dale Seymour.

Katzenback, J., & Smith, D. (1983). *The wisdom of teams: Creating the high-performance organization*. New York: HarperCollins.

Kellam, S. (1998, June 10). Quoted in research notes. *Education Week*, p. 30.

Kurcinka, M. (1991). *Raising your spirited child.* New York: HarperCollins.

Lindamood Bell Human Learning Management System. *The Lindamood Phoneme Sequencing (LiPS) Program.* San Louis Obispo, CA: Author.

McEwan, E. K. (1995). *Attention deficit disorder.* Wheaton, IL: Harold Shaw.

McEwan, E. K. (1996). *"I didn't do it": Dealing with dishonesty.* Wheaton, IL: Harold Shaw.

McEwan, E. K. (1998a). *The principal's guide to attention deficit hyperactivity disorder.* Thousand Oaks, CA: Corwin.

McEwan, E. K. (1998b). *How to deal with parents who are angry, troubled, afraid, or just plain crazy.* Thousand Oaks, CA: Corwin.

McEwan, E. K. (1998c). *The ADHD intervention checklist.* Thousand Oaks, CA: Corwin.

McGuinness, C., & McGuinness, G. (1998). *Reading reflex.* New York: Free Press.

Miller, J., Tansy, M., & Hughes, T. (1998). Functional behavioral assessment: The link between problem behavior and effective intervention in schools. *Current Issues in Education* [On-line]. Available: http://cie.ed.asu.edu/fall98/miller_tansy_huges/index.html

Mosteller, F., Light, R., & Sachs, J. (1996). Sustained inquiry in education: Lessons from skill grouping and class size. *Harvard Educational Review, 66*(4), 797-828.

Munk, D., & Repp, A. (1994). The relationship between instructional variables and problem behavior: A review. *Exceptional Children, 60*(5), 390-401.

Nelson, B. (1994). *1001 ways to reward employees.* New York: Workman.

O'Shea, D., O'Shea, L., & Rosenberg, M. (1998). *Student teacher to master teacher: A practical guide for educating students with special needs.* Upper Saddle River, NJ: Merrill.

Paine, S., Darch, C., Deutchman, L., Radicchi, J., & Rosellini, L. (1983). *Structuring your classroom for academic success.* Champaign, IL: Research Press.

Portner, J. (1998, October 21). Discipline problems linked to low scores, study says. *Education Week*, p. 6.

Slavin, R., Madden, N., & Dolan, L. (1996). *Every child, every school: Success for all.* Thousand Oaks, CA: Corwin.

Spalding, R. B., & Spalding, W. T. (1990).*The writing road to reading: The Spalding method of phonics for teaching speech, writing, and reading* (4th ed., rev.). New York: William Morrow.

Sprick, R. (1985). *Discipline in the secondary classroom: A problem-by-problem survival guide.* West Nyack, NY: The Center for Applied Research in Education.

Walker, H. (1979). *The acting-out child: Coping with classroom disruption.* Boston: Allyn & Bacon.

Walton, M. (1986). *The Deming management methods.* New York: Perigree.

CORWIN
PRESS

The Corwin Press logo—a raven striding across an open book—represents the happy union of courage and learning. We are a professional-level publisher of books and journals for K–12 educators, and we are committed to creating and providing resources that embody these qualities. Corwin's motto is "Success for All Learners."